792.027 Cummings, Richard,
CUM   1931-

          Simple makeup for
          young actors.

$12.95

DATE			

© THE BAKER & TAYLOR CO.

Simple Makeup for Young Actors

by RICHARD CUMMINGS

Illustrations by Melanie Carter

Boston   PLAYS, INC.   *Publishers*

Library of Congress Cataloging-in-Publication Data

Cummings, Richard, 1931–
    Simple makeup for young actors / by Richard Cummings.
        p.   cm.
    Includes bibliographical references.
    Summary: Discusses basic theatrical makeup and how it can be used
to transform the actor into many different characters.
    ISBN 0-8238-0290-6 : $10.00
    1. Make-up, Theatrical. [1. Makeup, Theatrical.] I. Title.
PN2068.C87   1990
792'.027—dc20   89-23118
                                                                     CIP
                                                                      AC

MANUFACTURED IN THE UNITED STATES OF AMERICA

CONTENTS

Simple Makeup
for
Young Actors

Introduction

The first makeup was probably a smear of white clay across the face of a caveman or woman. As it is with primitive peoples today, such decoration can be for magical or comic effect or to attract a romantic glance. Masks were used for the same purposes and became standard equipment for performers in the formal Greek and Roman theatres and were used well into the Middle Ages, sometimes along with painted makeup.

But in Shakespeare's Elizabethan times, stage masks were almost entirely replaced by powder and paint. Early face paints used cheap clay colors, charcoal blacks, and vegetable dyes mixed with oils or sometimes crude animal fat. Many an impoverished Elizabethan actor smeared his face with ham rind before patting on powdered charcoal or pipe clay dust. That is how the expression "ham actor" came into being.

By the time of the Restoration, around 1660, women were allowed on the stage, and makeup began to be refined to make it more subtle and less dangerous to the complexion. Nonetheless, stark contrasts of light and dark were still necessary to keep facial features from fading away under the glaring gaslight. As chemistry became a science, pigments and creams were improved and made more comfortable and safe.

The first movie actors clung to the melodramatic makeup of the stage, but with new and more sensitive film, they eventually toned down their makeup. With the coming of sound in the 1920s, the sizzling carbon arc lamps were too noisy for the microphones, so silent and gentler incandescent electric lamps were developed, allowing actors to wear makeup that was even more subtle and closer to "natural." This new panchromatic makeup—sensitive to light of all colors—was then taken up by stage performers.

But the purpose of the theatre has never changed. The aim is still to make the audience believe that what they are seeing is real, whether it is a handsome man or woman, an exotic foreigner, or the Devil himself. And the problem of achieving that effect of reality under bright light and at a distance from the audience remains.

As commercial makeup has improved, it has become more expensive, too often putting it out of reach of the amateur or beginning professional performer. Fortunately, the cosmetics used for everyday makeup have also improved, are relatively low in price, and are available at most drugstores and cosmetic counters. Modern artificial fibers are used to make acceptable wigs and beards. Cheap makeup and three-dimensional makeup pieces are easy to come by, particularly around Halloween.

You can easily and inexpensively assemble a basic makeup kit from materials found around the home and at the cosmetics counter. And, as you read through the instructions and practice the exercises in this book, you will soon be prepared to create makeup for just about any role you undertake in a school or community theatre play, historical or religious pageant, film, video, or just for fun.

1
Makeup Kit

D on't try to create your makeup kit all at once. From the listings
below choose only the materials and tools you need imme-
diately, and collect the other items as each new acting part and
makeup challenge comes along.

Basic kit

You can assemble a basic makeup kit for straight and glamorous
makeup and some character makeup by making relatively inexpensive purchases at a good cosmetics counter. Many of the materials in
a professional kit (see page 7) are more expensive and must be
purchased from a theatrical supply house or by mail from makeup
manufacturers. The makeup kits available in variety stores around
Halloween are inexpensive and can add special materials to your
basic kit, such as greasepaint makeup, nose putty, crepe hair and
spirit gum.

A shoe box or large cigar box will hold your basic kit. Later you
may want to buy a small fishing tackle box with one or two swing-out
trays for the smaller items.

For your first projects try using cake makeup, available at all
cosmetics counters. It must be applied carefully and quickly with a
sponge, but it needs no powdering and it is available in a great
variety of colors.

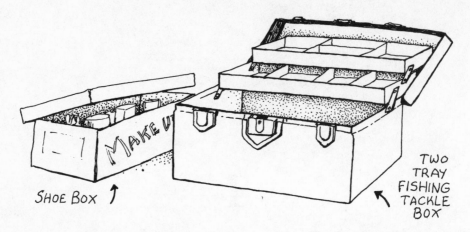

SHOE BOX

TWO
TRAY
FISHING
TACKLE
BOX

The foundation or makeup base goes on first, before rouge, highlights, eye makeup, and other details are added. Because manufacturers are continually changing the names and numbers of their foundation shades, it is not possible to direct you to a specific brand and its code listings. Look for a large cake makeup compact with three foundation colors: one from a pink group, one from an ivory group, and one from a peach group. To the eye they will appear as skin colors of predominantly red, yellow, and orange tints. The compacts often include a brush or two, a mirror, and an assortment of smaller cakes of makeup including flesh-tone liner colors and the more vivid eye shadow colors. In one package you get the foundations and eye shadow you need for straight and glamorous makeup as well as some liner colors needed for character makeup. Of course, buying two different compacts gives you a greater choice of shades.

DIMESTORE HALLOWEEN
MAKE-UP KIT

LARGE COMPACT

To complete your basic kit you need at least one of the following, if it is not included in your large compact:

sponge

eyebrow pencil

black mascara and applicator

rouge

lipstick

cleansing cream

cleansing tissues

For detailed advice on choosing the above materials, read on about the more diverse types of makeup and tools available for a professional kit.

Professional kit

The best container for a professional makeup kit is a large, two- or three-tray plastic fishing tackle box. Some performers affix a mirror to the inside of the box lid for use on those occasions when there is no dressing room mirror—or no dressing room!

Cleansing materials

Cream and liquid makeup removers or inexpensive cold cream are adequate for preparing your skin for makeup and for cleaning off makeup after a performance. Actors with sensitive skin may choose to purchase products designed for their skin types, or those marked "hypoallergenic." Actors with acne or similar skin problems should use anti-bacterial products to avoid irritation or infection.

Basic and professional kits should include plenty of cleansing tissues and a small hand towel.

The tissues are for use with removal cream. The hand towel is for drying the face after the makeup has been removed and the face washed. A complete professional kit also includes cotton balls for applying skin tonic or astringent and liquid makeup. Cotton swabs are helpful for removing smudged mascara and making minor changes. Eye makeup remover pads are helpful for removing heavy eye makeup and also for fixing small mistakes. Keep a small bowl of water handy to dampen cake makeup, moisten cotton balls, and clean your finger tips as you work.

In addition to cake makeup, most professionals choose from the variety of makeup types listed below. As you will see, each type has its advantages and its drawbacks.

Greasepaint

Even the least expensive professional greasepaint provides a range of makeup, including foundation colors, lining colors, and character colors. It is packaged as relatively hard sticks wrapped in paper. Suppliers offer a limited range of skin tones, but those can be mixed to produce just about any foundation you are ever likely to need. They must be applied with care to avoid either streaking or a mask-like, caked look.

Soft greasepaint, which comes in tubes, pots, or jars, can be applied more quickly than hard greasepaint, but it is a bit more expensive. It can be shiny if you do not powder it well after application.

Cream stick

Cream sticks are more expensive than greasepaint but are used extensively by professionals because they come in a wider variety of foundation colors, are non-greasy, and hold up well for long periods under lights. Some cream-stick makeup is available at cosmetics counters.

Liquid makeup

Professional liquid makeups are made to be applied to large areas, mainly for body painting. The liquid foundations are good enough for basic use, but use the darker foundation tones whenever possible, because they are made for day use and turn pale under theatrical lighting.

Cake makeup

As noted, day-use cake makeup is inexpensive, readily available, and comes in a broad range of shades. Film and video actors favor cake makeup because it never runs under lights. Professional cake makeup is more expensive than the cosmetics counter variety but is

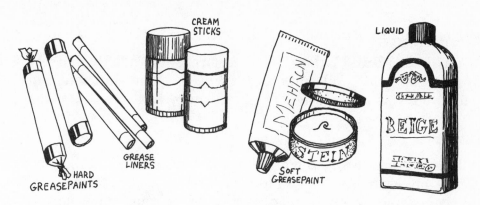

CREAM STICKS

LIQUID

HARD GREASEPAINTS

GREASE LINERS

SOFT GREASEPAINT

BEIGE

better adapted to theatrical lighting. It doesn't have to be powdered after application, and because it is greaseless and water-soluble, it is easy to remove. One drawback: Cake makeup dries quickly and the colors are not as easy to mix as greasepaint and cream makeup. That means you must take more care in choosing your foundation colors, since they can't be so easily adjusted by mixing.

Liners

Lining colors are used for adding facial detail after the foundation has been applied. These liners come in hard and soft greasepaint sticks or small pots. Professional lining colors are available in a wide range, including a variety of reds used as lip color or for novelty and fantasy makeup. (For basic kits, regular lipstick is adequate in most instances.)

Eye liners found at cosmetics counters come in every imaginable color, including silvers and golds and phosphorescent colors, and can be used for applying facial lines (worry lines, wrinkles, etc.). They are good enough for a basic kit, but try to include black or dark brown, and ivory or white for highlighting or toning down other colors.

Eyebrow pencils

Wooden eyebrow pencils are best; make sure you have both black and dark brown. Those that you can buy in any drugstore are fine for a basic kit. Professional eyebrow pencils are only longer and therefore a bit easier to handle.

Eye makeup: mascara and eye shadow

You'll need both black and dark brown water-soluble mascara and eye shadow of several tints, depending on your skin tone and the effect you wish to achieve.

Rouge

This cheek coloring comes in many shades of red. Cake rouge is patted on with a sponge. Powdered rouge is brushed on with a blusher brush or rouge mop. Any kind of rouge may be used by amateurs or professionals.

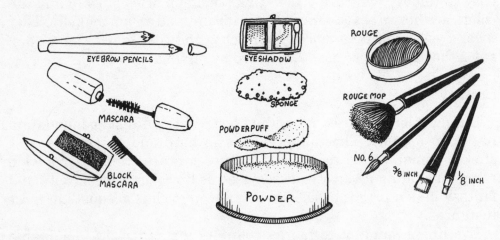

Powder

Powder sets your foundation and dulls greasy shine. Although you can use baby powder for a basic kit, it tends to give a white mask effect. Translucent powders are better for basic and professional use. They can be applied over any foundation or finished makeup without altering the color.

Powder puffs

Powder puffs often come with the boxes of translucent powder or can be purchased separately. The round, flat velour powder puffs, which can be washed and reused many times, are best.

Sponges

Plastic foam sponges are used for applying cake, cream, and greasepaint foundations.

Brushes

Narrow liner brushes and broader rouge brushes often come with eye liner and other compact kits. If possible, also include a ⅛-inch flat brush for detail and a ⅜-inch flat brush for blending. Short-haired sable brushes are best, and a longer handle gives you better control. Eventually you can add a ¼-inch flat brush for highlights and shadows, numbers 2 and 6 filberts for detail, and a pony hair rouge mop for patting on powdered rouge. The better cosmetics counters usually offer a variety of brushes, which are often as good as those available from theatrical supply companies.

Special materials

The special cosmetics items that follow can be expensive, so it is best to acquire them only as needed, rather than invest in all of them at once.

False eyelashes

Any good cosmetics department has a variety of lashes—black and brown are the most commonly needed. False eyelashes should be thick enough to be visible under theatrical light from a distance, but not so thick that they cast shadows over the eyes. For comic false eyelashes, see clown makeup in Chapter 7.

Crepe wool and spirit gum

Crepe wool, or artificial hair, comes in braided ropes and is available from theatrical supply houses in colors from dead white to flaming red and even green. (See Chapter 4.) It is often available in variety stores during the Halloween season, as are wigs and simple makeup kits.

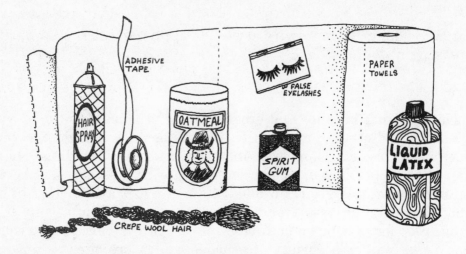

Crepe hair is attached to the skin with spirit gum and latex, both available through theatrical supply houses. For temporary use, as with Halloween makeup, you can substitute light corn syrup as an adhesive.

Nose putty and mortician's wax

Nose putty and mortician's wax (sold under several brand names, of which the best known is Derma-wax) are professional materials usually acquired through a theatrical supply house or from a manufacturer, but may be more readily available at Halloween. They are used to build up noses and other features by sculpting. (See Chapter 6.)

Hair spray

Hair spray is used to secure chignons and falls and to hold the shape of dressed hair and wigs. (See Chapter 4.) Hair pins, clips, barrettes, and combs are also useful for arranging hair.

Miscellaneous

Tooth wax is used to black out teeth and give a snaggle-toothed effect. Orange sticks and wire modeling tools are handy for sculpting three-dimensional features from nose putty or Derma-wax. Scissors and single-edged razor blades are useful for sharpening eyebrow pencils and cutting out paper templates for masking skin surfaces during various makeup procedures. As you will see in Chapters 6 and 7, there are specialized uses for such odd items as moleskin, starched gauze, oatmeal, collodion, false eyelids, and even puffed rice.

Makeup table

Your basic makeup station can be as simple as a table with a mirror and two unshaded lamps with 100-watt bulbs positioned on either side and equidistant to cast a balanced light on your face. A three-paneled mirror gives a better all-around view of your face. The fully professional makeup station features ten 40-watt bulbs spaced around the top and sides of the mirror, but it is a lucky amateur actor, indeed, who has such an elaborate set-up. Finally, you need a large washable makeup bib, a robe or plastic shoulder cape to protect your costume, and a wastebasket for used cleanup pads, cotton balls, and other articles. Keep paper towels handy for general cleanup of the makeup area.

Now for your first exercise: "Straight Makeup."

2

Straight Makeup

The main purpose of straight makeup is to maintain a normal daytime look under theatrical lighting, which is different from natural sunlight and from most indoor light. Of course, most actors like to improve their appearance a little while they are at it, and you will find directions for such corrective or "glamour" makeup in the next chapter.

However, an understanding of straight makeup application is necessary before you move on to more advanced work.

The skull

The shape and surface modeling of the human face are to a large extent determined by the skull. The high spots of the skull determine the parts of the face that will reflect more light and make such features prominent. Likewise, the hollow places will absorb more light and therefore be shadowed and will seem to recede.

Study the front and profile views of the skull in the illustration. Then run your fingers over your own face, starting at the forehead, then feeling the slight depression between it and the browbone. Notice the way the outside of the eye socket runs down to the bulging cheekbone.

No two faces are alike because each has its own bone structure. Makeup cannot change that shape, but you can use makeup to improve or modify it.

Color

What we think of as our natural skin coloring is really the result of how pigments in our skin and blood reflect a particular brightness and quality of light. Under sunlight, a florid or reddish-pink complexion absorbs most of the yellows and blues and greens of the sun's spectrum but bounces the red back to our eyes. If an actor decides to tone down his naturally florid coloring by using a yellowish foundation, and then steps onto a stage lighted with strong yellow filters, yellow cancels yellow and the actor's face takes on a ghostly white look. Under stage lights with blue, green, or violet filters, certain makeups become nearly black. The wrong lighting color can have a similarly disastrous effect on eye and lip makeup. Because most modeling of highlights and shadows is done with neutral brown and gray makeup, that aspect of facial makeup is not so strongly affected by lighting.

Adjusting makeup to the many patterns of filter and lights is complex and highly technical. Fortunately, most stage lighting is dominated by flesh pinks and/or amber filters, both of which are flattering to most makeups. Nonetheless, it is always a good idea to test your makeup under the lighting that will be used. If your makeup does not "read," that is, look as you had expected, change it or consult a lighting or makeup expert.

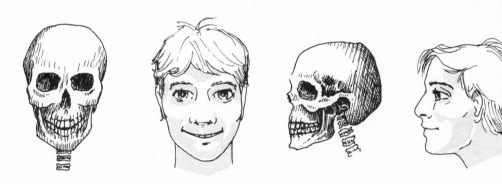

FACIAL BONE STRUCTURE

Mixing makeup color

There are two basic ways to approach makeup application. The traditional method is to select from a variety of pre-mixed shades, starting with a foundation and applying the various shadows and liner colors on top of that basic "mask." A more contemporary method is to start with only three primary colors in cake makeup and "mix" them on the face; for example, applying a yellow eye shadow first, then a touch of blue to produce a greenish effect. Most makeup artists use a combination of the two approaches.

To be successful at any combination of application methods, you must have a basic understanding of how color works.

We see color in three basic hues or primaries: red, yellow, and blue. When two primary colors are mixed, the result is a related secondary color. For example, when yellow and blue are blended, green results, and is their secondary color. Mix red and yellow to get orange. Blue and red mixed become violet or purple.

The best way to understand the relationships between colors is to visualize them in a kind of circular rainbow: a color wheel. If you

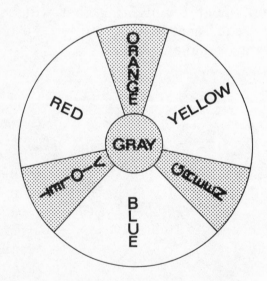

COLOR WHEEL

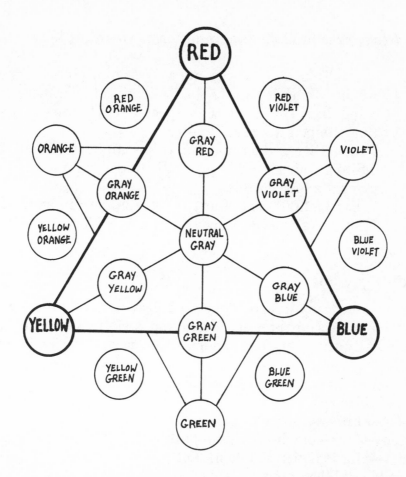

COLOR SPECTRUM SUBDIVISIONS

draw a circle and position each of the three primary colors inside it, you can then fit the secondary colors between their appropriate parent primaries, as shown in the color wheel illustration. The illustration above shows the complex relationship between a broader range of subdivisions of the color spectrum. Mixing one primary with one secondary color in varying proportions produces subtle differences. Both pink and maroon are mixtures of red and blue, but pink has more red while maroon has more blue.

Notice that a mixture of all colors produces gray, as seen at the center of both charts.

There are three fundamental color terms you must learn:

- *Hue:*   Color. That is, it represents a particular point on the color wheel, whether that is the basic wheel or a more complicated diagram of the color spectrum. The hue is the color that can be altered in quality.
- *Value:* The quality of the color. The value can be altered by adding white or black. White gives the hue a higher value. Black gives it a lower value.
- *Shade:* A particular shade of any color results from adding black. It shadows or dulls and darkens a hue. Maroon is a shade of red.

Foundation color

As mentioned, manufacturers do not provide reliable color names and code numbers for their ever-changing varieties of hue and shade. But generally there are six generic color categories for foundation makeup:

Ivory—white-yellow with a hint of blue
Pink—white-red
Peach—white-yellow-red
Creamy-beige—medium orange-pink
Florid—pinkish with red dominant
Light tan—yellow-brown

Note the hues that make up each category of foundation and affect their values. Some manufacturers use one or more of these categories in listing their foundations, some do not. But comparison of the hue components with what you actually see in the makeup will give you an idea of what to look for in our gallery makeup charts, which use mostly the above foundation categories. One example: If a foundation seems to have a high value of red but is not dominantly red, it is more likely to belong to the pink group than it is to belong in the florid category.

CAKE MAKEUP

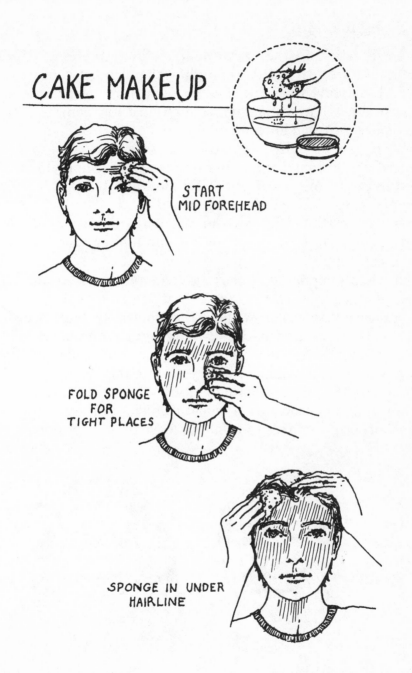

START
MID FOREHEAD

FOLD SPONGE
FOR
TIGHT PLACES

SPONGE IN UNDER
HAIRLINE

19

Applying makeup

We will stick to the traditional method, applying a pre-mixed foundation first, then the highlights, then the eyeshadow and liner colors. Let's start with cake makeup, which is inexpensive and readily available. Liquid makeup, though also inexpensive and easy to find, is less suitable for eye makeup and detail.

Hair should be pulled away from the face, and the skin thoroughly cleansed. Men should shave an hour or so before applying makeup. If the skin is very oily, clean with skin tonic or after-shave. If the skin is very dry, apply a bit of moisturizer.

Wipe a moistened foam cosmetic sponge over the surface of the cake in circular strokes, getting enough makeup to cover the whole face and throat.

Start applying foundation at the center of the forehead, stroking to each side then upward, taking care not to get any makeup on the hair itself, but working color in under the roots of the hairline. Next cover the cheeks, chin, and neck, stroking lightly and smoothly. For the hollows around the eyes, corners of the mouth, and down the side of the nose, fold the sponge around your forefinger.

Now wet the sponge again, squeeze out excess water, and swiftly blend the foundation into a smooth finish, fading it down the neck with feathering strokes so as not to leave an abrupt line of color.

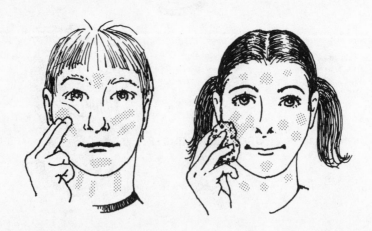

GREASEPAINT APPLICATION

20

Greasepaint

Hard greasepaint goes on more smoothly if the skin is first coated with a thin film of cold cream. Peel the covering off the greasepaint stick and apply light strokes to the forehead, cheeks, nose, chin, and throat. Then, using your finger tips, blend the makeup over your face and neck. If you are mixing two or more foundation colors, apply parallel strokes of each color and then blend, rather than applying one color over the other.

Soft greasepaint is already creamy, so no cold cream base is needed beforehand, unless the skin is very dry. Using your fingers or a sponge, space small dots over the face, then blend gently and evenly, fading down the neck and up into the hairline. Avoid getting any makeup on the hair.

If the coating is too thick, blend it again with your fingers, picking up the excess and wiping it off on a tissue until a finger drawn across the makeup doesn't pick up any more.

Cream stick

Apply this in strokes at forehead, cheeks, chin, and neck, then blend with a damp sponge. If you need more color, apply the stick directly to the sponge, then dab on and blend.

Liquid

Using a dry sponge, work the liquid quickly over the forehead and other areas of the face, using the same technique as with cake makeup. If you need extra color, dab it on and blend, as with the cream stick.

Rouge

A good sense of the shape and position of your cheekbones will help when applying rouge. Place several dots of cream rouge along the sloped prominence of the cheekbone. Then with your finger tip, blend the cream in small, circular movements along the slope of the bone to the ridge above the deep hollow. Clean your finger on tissue, then blend the edges to give a soft flush whose center is at the highest point of the cheekbone. Avoid applying rouge as a solid circle of color, unless you want a comic, overly made-up effect.

Highlights and shadows can be added next, but they are not necessary in simple straight makeup. They are described in Chapter 3.

Powder

Before setting the makeup and reducing shine with powder, you must make sure you have a smooth foundation finish. If you find that the makeup has squeezed out of the natural creases at the corners of your eyes and down the side of the nose, gently stretch the skin to open the lines, then use a sponge or finger to smooth the makeup into the lines.

Next, gather plenty of powder on the rougher side of your velour powder puff. Then fold the puff around the powder and roll it with thumb and forefinger, spreading the powder evenly in the fibers of the puff. Open the puff again and start patting the powder gently onto the makeup, working from the bottom of one ear in a circle around the face and in toward the nose. Do not rub with the puff; dab powder on gently. To get an even finish in the areas around the eyes, mouth, and nose, use an outside segment of the puff, slightly folded.

Greasepaint foundation should be powdered at least twice after application, cream stick and liquid at least once. Don't spare the powder. Any excess can be brushed away with a clean rouge mop or blush brush kept just for this purpose. It is not necessary to powder cake makeup after application unless the skin is very greasy, in which case a little light powdering will reduce any shininess.

Eye makeup

Start with the eyebrows. Black and brown pencils are the most commonly used to enhance natural eyebrows and keep stage lights from "bleaching" them out of existence. If you are a redhead or a blonde, you may want to mix brown with short, fine strokes of a rust or amber pencil. Use a single-edged razor blade to sharpen the pencil to a flat, chisel-like point. Using the sharp edges of this chisel, draw hair-like strokes, following the natural shape of the eyebrow. See A

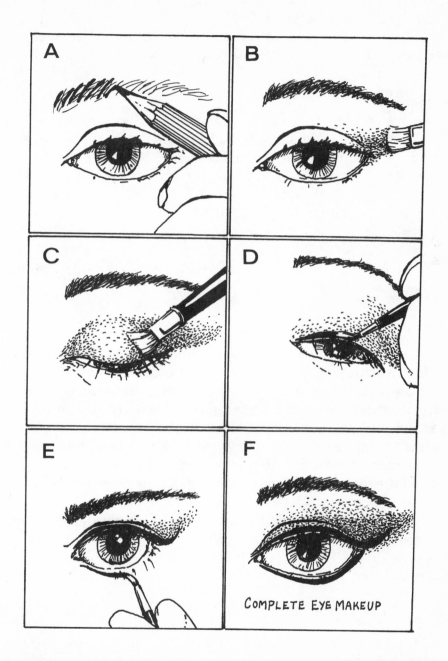

COMPLETE EYE MAKEUP

in the illustration. Do not draw a single, unbroken line, unless you want that hard, "made-up" effect.

See Chapter 3 for blocking out eyebrows for corrective or character makeup.

Eye shadow

Cake or powder eye shadow is inexpensive and easy to find. Apply to eyelid with the brush provided or with a ¼-inch professional brush, B, C in illustration. If you use more than one shadow shade, use a separate brush for each so the colors won't muddy to gray.

To get a more interesting color combination, first outline the eye shadow pattern with a cosmetic pencil (not an eyebrow pencil) of one shade, then fill in with cake or powder shadow of a slightly different shade.

Greasepaint liners or cream makeup may also be used, but they must be powdered carefully afterward to set them.

Eye liner

Cake liners are easiest to come by and to use. Cosmetic eye-liner pencils are also good, but the liner must be powdered afterward.

To apply cake liner, moisten your brush, then swirl it in the cake until it is loaded with color. To bring the brush to a fine point, draw it across the cake and twirl it slowly at the same time.

To line the upper lid, tilt your head back and look down, watching in the mirror. Draw a line along the root of the lashes, D, to the outer corner of the eye, then up and tapering out, as shown in the illustration.

Tilt your head down to do the lower lid, looking up so you can draw under the lower lashes, as illustrated, E, F.

Mascara

Make sure the applicator brush is covered completely with mascara: Plunge it all the way into the tube, then wipe the tip of the brush against the rim of the tube to remove any excess. If using block mascara, wet the brush with warm water and work up a moist cream on the block. For the upper lashes, tilt your head back and look down.

Apply the mascara first with sideways strokes of the brush, then with the brush parallel to the lashes to separate them. Tilt your chin down and roll your eyes up to do the lower lashes. Let each coating dry, adding more mascara until you have the density of color desired.

Lips

The lip brushes sold at cosmetics counters are adequate, but a #6 professional brush is better. Using a lipstick, or a cake or cream liner, load the brush with color, then twirl the brush slowly on the side of your hand to bring it to a fine point. First outline the mouth, then fill in the shape of top and bottom lips. For a softer look or for male makeup, use only a little color applied with the finger.

Blot the mouth with tissue to take off any extra color.

To enlarge the lips or make them smaller or a different shape, see Chapter 3.

Removal of makeup

Put some cold cream or skin lotion on your hands, rub it onto your face, then wipe off makeup with tissues. Don't rub so hard as to irritate the skin; instead, try another application of cream. Two or three applications may be necessary to remove complicated makeups.

Afterward, wash your face gently but thoroughly with warm water and soap, then dry.

Some actors prefer baby oil or light mineral oil to cold cream. Liquid removers are equally effective, and there is a variety of professional removers available from makeup manufacturers.

Removal of hairpieces and latex prosthetic pieces held in place with spirit gum calls for careful use of acetone or special spirit gum remover. (See Chapters 5 and 6.)

Actors with skin problems should follow up removal with application of antibacterial lotions.

Makeup for black actors

For a long time there was no special makeup for actors of color and little instruction in addressing their makeup needs. Now professional makeup manufacturers have begun to offer special foundations for dark skin, and several cosmetics manufacturers offer full lines of cosmetics for blacks, as well as detailed instructions on how to use them.

In general, the black actor or actress needs a foundation that is a tone lighter than the skin. For darker skins, browns containing strong reddish tones should be used. To darken a light brown complexion, use a brown containing medium reddish tones. Highlights should be much lighter than the natural skin tone and contain golden yellow. There is seldom a danger that theatrical lights will bleach out the black artist's skin, but the wrong foundation makeup can. Avoid the light browns; they contain a lot of white and can give a chalky look. The above suggestions for a reddish tone to the foundation and a strong yellow in highlights gives dark skin a special luster, rather than muddying it.

Spread the foundation as thinly as possible so that its reds or yellow-golds brighten the appearance. At the same time, make sure the natural tone shows through, the brightness "floating" on the natural color.

Lips should be colored a stronger red than their natural color, but use reds with a higher value (brighter) only if you want to enlarge the lips. Outlining just inside the natural shape can help reduce the size of the lips.

An uneven or slightly blotched natural complexion can be smoothed out with the use of a face glosser or "gleamer" which has iridescent qualities. These gleamers are usually included in cosmetics lines for blacks. Iridescent eyeliner for actresses, particularly in silver or yellow-gold, can bring more brightness when applied to the upper lids. For men, a much more subtle touch of metallic eye shadow can help, but use it sparingly.

Use very dark brown or black eyebrow pencils for the eyes. Powder only if you are using greasepaint, and then no more than is necessary to prevent any perspiration from beading the makeup.

3
Corrective Makeup

More often than not, the actor who will appear as himself or herself on stage will be required to look more attractive, or a little different, younger or older. Character makeup involves more elaborate distortion of the actor's normal look, but both corrective (or glamour) and character makeup get their effects by sculpting with paint, using basic principles of light and shade as well as optical illusions like these:

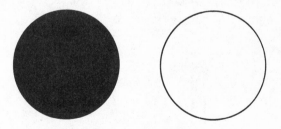

Illusion One: Of the two circles in the illustration, the black one appears smaller, although both are actually the same size. This is because black reflects less light than white and is a recessive color. It seems to withdraw and to shrink, particularly when compared to a similar white shape. If you want an area of the face to seem recessed, use a darker shade of makeup. If you want to emphasize a prominent feature, like the tip of the nose, highlight it with a lighter shade of makeup.

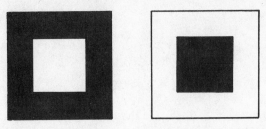

Illusion Two: Place a white area on a black background and a black area on a white background. The white on black area will seem much larger and closer to you than the black on white. You are making double use of the light/dark principle. At the same time that the white square seems to protrude, the black background recedes, making the white seem even bigger and closer.

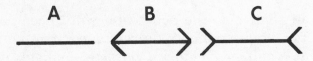

Illusion Three: All three of the horizonal lines in the illustration are the same length, yet the second seems shorter than the third. The acute, arrow-point angles at either end of B draw the eye's attention inward toward the center of the line and make it seem shorter. The open angles at either end of C draw the attention outward and open it up, seeming almost to stretch the line.

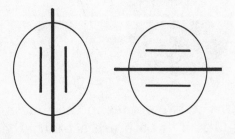

Illusion Four: Both ovals are the same size and shape, but the one with the lines drawn up and down seems a bit longer and narrower, while the one with the lines drawn across it seems broader. Lines and shadows drawn horizontally across a face make it seem wider and a bit flat. Vertical lines and shadows make a face seem longer and narrower.

28

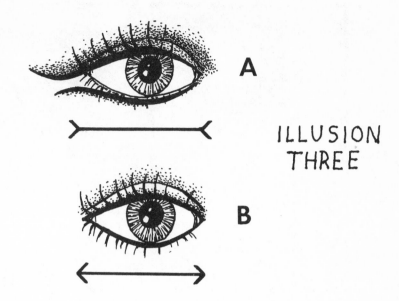

ILLUSION
THREE

Using the Illusions

Eye makeup makes the most effective use of all these optical illusions. Both eyes in the illustration are the same size, but A appears longer than B because of the liner that extends above and below the eye, just as the open angles at the end of the straight line in Illusion Three seem to make the line longer.

Illusions One and Two can be useful for making the white of the eye seem larger by surrounding it with darker shadow on the eyelids. The eye can be made to seem smaller by surrounding the eye with a lighter tone of paint, making the brow and upper cheekbone seem to protrude while the eye recedes.

The ideal face

Though very rare, the face with perfectly balanced and harmonious features is considered to be ideal. In the ideal face, the space between the inner corners of the eyes is the width of one eye. The inner ends of the eyebrows are separated by a space a bit less than an eye's width, and the mouth is slightly wider than the width of an eye.

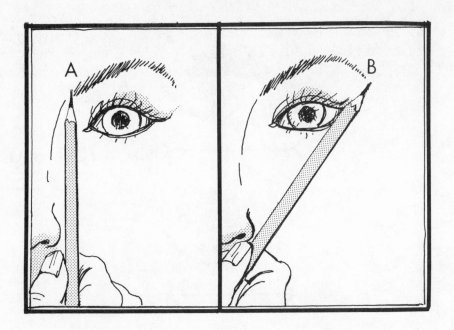

THE PERFECT EYEBROW

The point of an eyebrow pencil held beside the nose and straight up marks the inner end of the eyebrow, A. If the same pencil is then angled over from the side of the nostril and across the outer corner of the eye, the tip of the pencil will mark the outside end of the perfect eyebrow, B.

It is this set of proportions as well as a look of general good health that you are aiming for as you apply corrective makeup to improve your natural appearance.

Corrective foundation

If your complexion is uneven, use a heavier application of foundation color, using a moist sponge to dab or stipple it evenly over the skin. Under stage lighting, this pattern of almost infinitesimally tiny dots of color effectively screens any larger irregularities or spottiness of your natural skin color. The same applies to freckles and blemishes, although you must avoid so thick a coating of makeup that the foundation looks like a mask.

Shadows under the eyes can be concealed with cream or cake foundation slightly lighter in color than the foundation base. There are also special cover creams available. Apply the lighter highlights to the naturally dark areas, then blend carefully with the finger tip.

Wide face and thin face

Keeping in mind the bone structure of your face, you can change the overall impression by using the principles of light and dark. To slim a face that is too wide or full, choose makeup a shade or two darker than your foundation and fill in the hollow under the cheekbone and blend into the foundation with your finger. Then highlight the area on the cheekbone above the hollow with a shade lighter than your foundation. This will give depth and an appearance of angular boniness to a face that is otherwise broad and bland, see A, B. Cake rouge can be added for color, lighter on the highlighted area, blending to darker red in the shaded area.

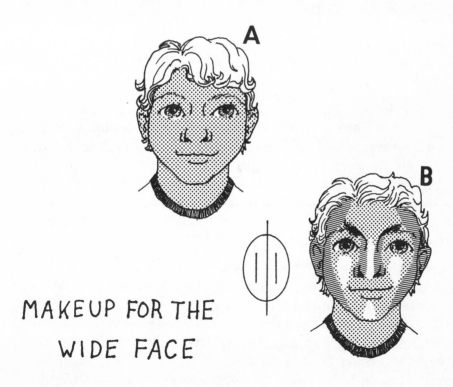

MAKEUP FOR THE
WIDE FACE

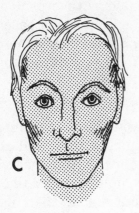

C

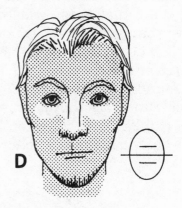

D

MAKEUP FOR THE
THIN FACE

A face that is too thin or gaunt and bony can be modified by reversing these principles. Instead of deepening the hollow under the cheekbone by darkening it, C, use a lighter shade to bring it out, D, at the same time reducing the highlight on the cheekbone or, better yet, adding no highlight at all to the foundation color. The bony features then appear to retreat, seeming to smooth out the face.

Jawline, chin, and forehead

To strengthen a weak jawline, make an almost right-angled shadow from just below the ear down the neck and blend it in under the chin with a darker foundation shade or a brownish cake shadow, as shown, A, page 34. Emphasize this alteration by using a lighter shade of makeup to highlight above the artificial jawline, blending it carefully.

A receding chin can be made more prominent if you highlight the tip; a chin that is too prominent can be made less so with the application of a shadow darker than the foundation.

A high forehead can be lowered by adding a strip of darker shading along the top of the forehead, close to the hairline, B. This blends with the hair shadow and has the effect of making the brow smaller and lowering the hairline.

If the forehead is too low, reverse the principle and use a lighter shade to blend a highlight along the hairline. If the forehead bulges too much, shade each temple so the shadows in effect "squeeze" the brow in from either side and make it seem smoother and narrower.

Noses

A nose that is too broad can be narrowed by shading down each side and over the nostrils, then highlighting straight down the bridge of the nose, as shown, C.

A nose that is too short will seem longer if you run a highlight down the center and over and under the tip, with the highlight brightest on the tip.

A nose that is too long can be made to look shorter by putting shadow darker than the foundation just under the tip, blended slightly up over the top, as shown, D. The shadow thus created will make the end of the nose recede and the whole nose will seem shorter.

To straighten a crooked nose, use light and dark shading to paint a very straight nose, shaded up each side, highlighted in a straight swath down the center bridge.

Mouths

Male actors should underplay their lip makeup, avoiding extreme changes and using subtle, brownish lip colors or a brown eye pencil rather than brilliant colors. Women can use bolder, brighter lipstick shades.

To enlarge thin lips, use the application technique described in Chapter 2 to draw outside the natural lip outline. Do not alter the shape itself; just follow the natural outline of the mouth to make it larger.

CORRECTING FACIAL FEATURES

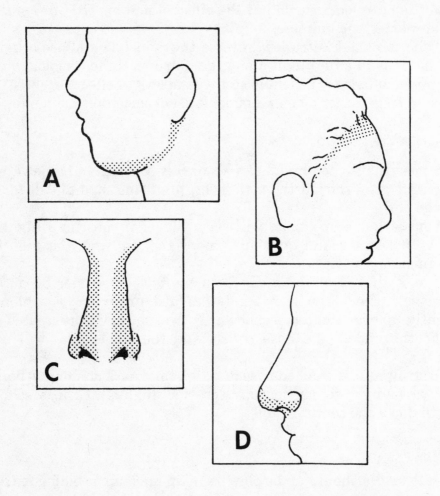

A – WEAK JAWLINE   B – HIGH FOREHEAD
C – BROAD NOSE   D – LONG NOSE

To reduce thick lips, apply the base foundation so that it edges over the natural outline of the lips. Then paint a new, smaller outline inside the normal outline. Again, avoid changing the basic outline unless a burlesque or grotesque effect is desired.

If you want to make the mouth wider, you can extend the outline a bit beyond the corners, and to correct a mouth that is too wide, cover the outer corners with foundation and draw in a new lip outline.

Correcting eyes and eyebrows

Optical illusions come into play in eye makeup by adjusting accents with eye liner and eye shadow. Small eyes can be enlarged by opening up the eye liner outlines. Deep-set eyes will seem more prominent with a light-and-shade combination of heavier eye shadow and highlights just below the eyebrows.

Eyes too close together can be made to seem farther apart by drawing eye makeup out at the outer corners of the eyes, tightening makeup in close to the nose. Eyes set wide apart can appear closer together by reversing that pattern.

Drooping eyes can be given a lift by eye lining upwards at the outer corners. Prominent eyes can seem smaller or more recessed by eye lining darkly at the top and bottom and using strong highlights just beneath the eyebrows.

The perfectly shaped eyebrow starts just up from the inner corner of the eye, then follows the natural line of the browbone to about half an inch beyond the outer corner. Variations of this can be corrected with eyebrow pencil. Sparse eyebrows can be filled in, light eyebrows darkened, short eyebrows lengthened with the pencil.

If more extreme correction is necessary, you may have to block out the natural eyebrow before drawing in an entirely new one. The oldest and cheapest way to block out eyebrows is to rub a dampened bar of white or pale pink soap over the eyebrows to flatten them. Allow the soap to dry, cover with foundation and powder, then use your pencil to draw in that perfect eyebrow. Eyebrows can also be blocked out with clown white or zinc paste if the covering is powdered afterward, but both materials are less permanent than soap.

The best method is to brush spirit gum well into the eyebrows, stroking with the natural direction of the hair. When the gum covering is tacky, press the brows down with a damp cloth to spread the hairs flat. It may take several layers with powdering in between before makeup can be applied. Acetone or spirit gum remover will take off the blocking.

Mortician's wax (see Chapter 1) covers brows well and covers darker brows more readily than spirit gum. It will go on more firmly if you first coat the eyebrows with spirit gum, then apply the wax.

4

Hair and Wigs

Hair treatment is a vital element in makeup. It can enhance straight makeup or help turn the actor into an entirely different character. Hair styles can suggest personality, age, health, or the period called for by the play.

Natural hair

Restyling your own hair is the cheapest way to modify appearance. A good cut and style further alter the impression of straight makeup toward the ideal. The high forehead in the illustration, A, can be lowered by combing the hair forward into bangs and adding more hair body at the sides, B. One way to narrow a round face is to give

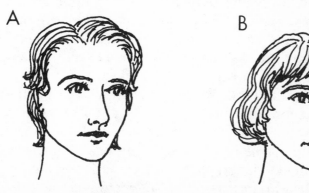

FEMALE HAIR STYLES

FEMALE
HAIR STYLES

the hair height on top. Hair styling can even change the look of a short neck, as in C, by drawing the hair up and exposing the neck. Or a long neck, as in D, can be made to seem shorter by bringing the hair in panels down below the jawline. A dozen other such tricks are well known to most hair stylists.

Male actors are more limited in hair styling for straight makeup. But the same principles apply. As indicated in the illustration, A, the length of the face can seem to change, depending on where the front hairline is. A high forehead can be lowered by combing the hair down or across the brow. A low forehead can be raised by combing the hair back from the brow. A receding hairline can be corrected by adding tiny, short strokes of an eyebrow pencil at the hairline, using a pencil the same color as the natural hair, B. Bald spots can be hidden with colored hairspray, cake makeup, or a special mascara called *masque*.

The tools and techniques used for hair styling are well known and described in many books on regular, day-use makeup. A good cosmetics counter often has free brochures on materials and devices available such as setting gels, sprays, foams, rollers, and curling irons.

Carefully combed and glossy hair suggests good health. Dull and lifeless hair indicates poor health and indifferent or non-existent styling.

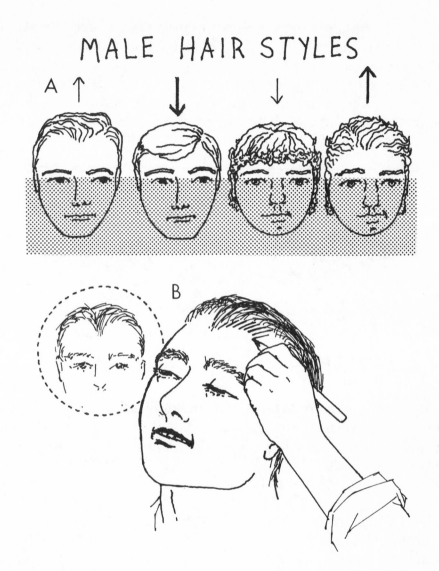

Coloring the hair

Young actors can color their hair gray to give an impression of middle or advanced age. The cheapest way to gray hair is to streak it with white powder or cornstarch, using a puff to apply the powder, then combing. But even if you protect your shoulders with a towel or makeup cape during application, powder tends to shake off onto your costume.

White cake makeup and liquid white mascara are good for streaking, to suggest middle age, or for character effects such as Dracula (see Chapter 7).

For a complete graying, liquid hair whitener is satisfactory. Sponge or brush it on a bit at a time, stroking along the natural direction of the hair growth, as in A. If the effect is too dull, spray on a little acrylic clear spray and comb it, leaving highlights.

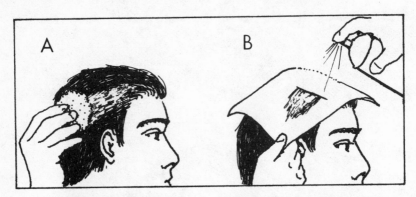

COLORING THE HAIR

White greasepaint or white stick makeup can also be used—especially for streaking over the ears—but it will rub off on hands, hats, and costumes. White shoe polish should not be used, as it is harmful to the scalp.

By far the best graying is achieved with temporary color hair sprays in aerosol cans. They come in a wide range of colors, including gold, silver, blue, pink, and green. Silver is best for graying.

To avoid getting spray on your makeup and costume, cover your shoulders with a towel or cape during application. Cut a piece of paper to follow your hairline and use it to protect your brow as you spray. To spray streaks or to tint just a lock or two, cut a slit in a sheet of paper, pull the lock through and spray as shown in the illustration, B.

Light hair can be made darker using the above materials and methods. But to make dark hair look lighter overall, it is usually necessary to have the hair lightened by a professional hair stylist first, then sprayed if a color tint is desired.

Soaping for baldness

You can create the effect of a receding hairline or of complete baldness with soap. First, soften soap flakes in water overnight. Better yet, partially submerge small bars of hand soap in water overnight, leaving the end of each bar dry so it will remain hard enough to grip. Apply the soap to the area of the hair you want to appear bald, treating a portion six inches across each time, B. Dry each layer with a hair dryer until the whole area is flattened, saturated, and smooth.

Finally, cut a portion the size of the bald area from a sheer, preferably flesh-colored nylon stocking. Using spirit gum, firmly seal the edge of the nylon to the forehead below the hairline, C. Then

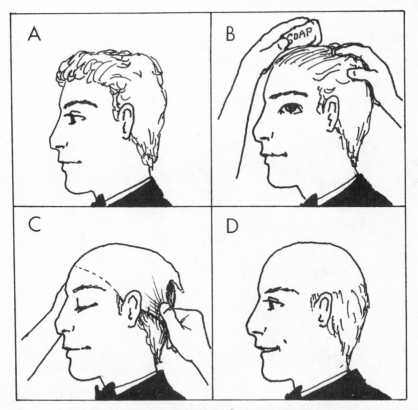

CREATING BALDNESS

stretch the nylon back over the soaped and flattened hair and the rest of the head, D. The nylon serves as a net, holding the soaped hair down and providing a good surface for makeup. Allow to dry thoroughly, then apply makeup matching your foundation color.

If you are aiming for a partially bald effect, stop the nylon at the point where you want the natural hair to appear. After applying makeup to the nylon, use an eyebrow pencil to draw many fine lines along the border between nylon and natural hair, simulating the roots of the hair at the edge of the balding area.

To remove, peel off the nylon and rinse the soap from your hair; apply a conditioner if necessary.

A more common method of imitating baldness is to cover the hair with a bald cap. This can be homemade or purchased from a theatrical supply house.

Hairpieces

Wigs and hairpieces offer even more possibilities for change. Female actors in straight makeup can benefit from the use of such hairpieces as switches, chignons, and falls. Switches of artificial hair

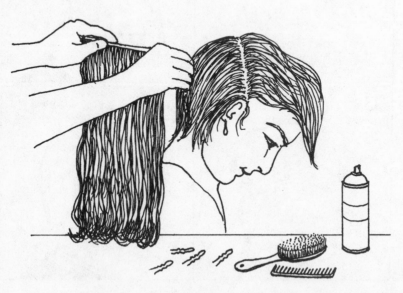

ATTACHING A HAIRPIECE

are sold in some variety stores and cosmetics departments. If you order real hair falls or switches from a wigmaker, be sure to send along a clipping of your own hair for a good color match.

Falls add loose flowing hair at the back of the head. To attach a fall, first part the hair across the back of the head from ear to ear, as shown in the illustration, combing the top hair forward temporarily. The hemmed straight edge of the fall is then pinned along the part and into the hair below the part. Finally, the front hair is combed back to cover the seam and held down with small hairpins.

Switches and chignons are simply pinned into place and do not have to be blended into the natural hair.

Readymade wigs

Real hair wigs are expensive, but they can be rented from theatrical supply or costume houses. Artificial hair wigs are sold around Halloween in variety stores and year-round from theatrical supply houses. You can often make your own wigs, as described later in this chapter.

Putting on a wig

Women and men with long hair must flatten their hair as much as possible before putting on a wig. Medium-length hair can be pinned flat to the scalp in small circular curls, A, page 44. Long hair should be wound around the head and pinned flat. Cover the hair with a cap made from a nylon stocking or pantyhose, knotted or sewn together at one end, B. Also, a length of elastic bandage can be wrapped around the head into a tight turban and pinned.

Both real and artificial hair wigs come with two types of hairline: hard-edge, or with a lace front or "blender." You can conceal the unnatural-looking front edge of a hard-edge wig by putting it on and then combing the wig hair forward in bangs or a fringe to cover the edge, D. Or comb a front fringe of your own hair out under the edge of the wig, then fold it back and blend it with the hair of the wig, fastening with pins if necessary.

The nylon net, lack, or gauze hairlines of blender wigs are affixed

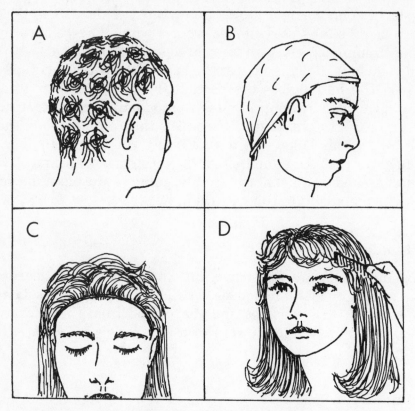

PUTTING ON A WIG

to the skin of the brow with spirit gum, then the front is covered with foundation color matching the forehead makeup.

If the wig has a gauze front, you can apply foundation makeup to the front edge of the wig before fixing the wig in place. Place a piece of waxed paper between the gauze and your own hair to keep the foundation makeup from sinking into the hair. Touch up the makeup on the gauze and powder until set. Then remove the wig and the paper, and powder the underside of the gauze to set it. You can now put the wig on again. To keep it from riding up on your forehead, lift the gauze with an ice cream stick or small spatula and slip a brush under it to apply spirit gum. Finally, using a dampened towel, firmly press along the full length of the leading edge to set the hairline in place. To remove wig, use spirit gum solvent.

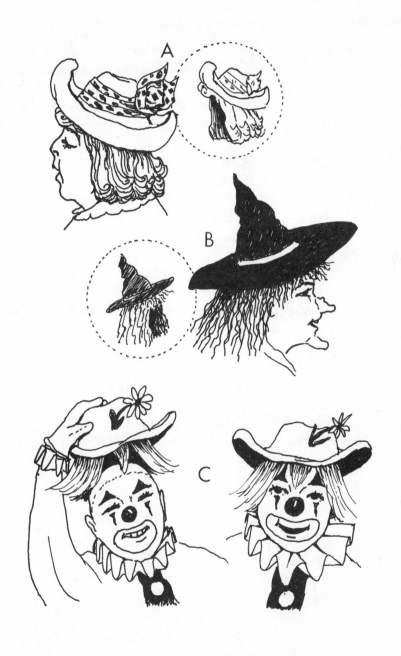

COMIC WIGS

Making your own wigs

Make-it-yourself wigs are most suitable for character and especially comic effects. The handiest and quickest method of making a wig is to attach real or artificial hair to the inside of a hat worn as part of the costume. Acrylic or crepe hair trailing out from under a witch's hat can give the proper scraggly appearance, B. False curls can be attached inside the brim of a bonnet, A. A clown's comic tufts can be attached to his hat, combed out and then sprayed with a fixative to hold their pointed shape, C.

A wig made from a clean yarn mop in its natural white color or dyed is best for clowns and rustic types, male or female, D. It can be attached inside the brim of a hat or sewn with heavy thread to form a full mop wig, as shown.

Fur pieces of assorted sizes and thicknesses can often be found at thrift shops and made into wigs by sewing them to hair nets or cloth caps. A strip of fur rigged with a rubber band, as shown in Chapter 5, can be used as fuzzy side hair under a hat or attached to the chin to make a comic beard.

You can make a full head wig or a partially bald wig by using spirit gum or glue to attach artificial hair or crepe wool hair to a cheap cotton net foundation.

For a half-bald wig, it is best to use a full head cap. A white or flesh-colored swimming or boating cap will serve if you cover its

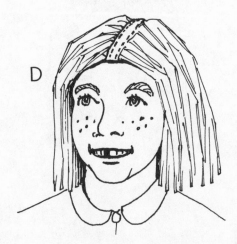

YARN-MOP
WIG

D

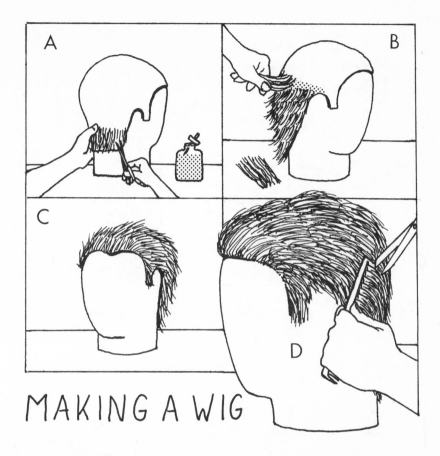

MAKING A WIG

seams with nose putty or mortician's wax, then cover the whole cap with foundation makeup.

For a completely bald head, flatten the natural hair, put on the cap, glue it along the browline and other edges with spirit gum, and then apply makeup to match your foundation color. To give the cap convincing texture, stipple it with your shadow color. You can even suggest veins and wisps of hair by drawing them in with your eyebrow pencil.

To build a full or partial wig on a latex or cloth cap, apply crepe wool hair in rows, "shingling" it from the nape of the neck up, as shown, A, B. Each glued layer overlaps the next. When you have finished "laying" the hair, trim it with scissors or electric clippers, D.

PERIOD HAIR STYLES

Period hair styles

The illustration shows some of the hair styles popular at various times in history. Some beard and mustache styles are shown in the next chapter. And you will find other period and ethnic hair and beard styles in our makeup gallery charts, Chapter 7.

A & B: Greco-Roman woman and man.

C & D: Elizabethan woman and man.

E & F: Seventeenth century woman and man.

G & H: Eighteenth century woman and man.

I & J: Nineteenth century woman and man.

K: 1920s woman.

L & M: 1930s woman and man.

N: 1950s woman.

O: 1960s man.

5
Beards and Mustaches

Professionally made beards and mustaches of real hair are expensive and usually must be ordered through a costume supply outlet, where they are available in all colors, shapes and sizes. You cannot get a good real-hair mustache for under thirty dollars and beards can cost hundreds. However, they can be and often are rented from costume houses for local productions, so the young actor should know how to use them.

Attaching a hairpiece

Real hair is knotted to a nylon base, which is affixed to the face with spirit gum; never use latex or another non-soluble glue, because it would make removal difficult and would ruin an expensive hairpiece.

First, hold the piece in position on your face so you can see where the spirit gum should be applied. Remove and brush a thin film of gum over the area, as shown, A. Allow to dry, then add a second coating. While the gum is still tacky, press the mustache or beard into position, paying special attention to the edges, which can be pressed firmly down with a dampened towel. If the beard extends up the side of the jaw, be sure to fit it under the natural sideburns, as shown, B. Comb or brush your natural hair down over the piece to conceal the seam. If there is still a gap between the hairpiece and your hairline, fill it in with crepe wool hair, attached with spirit gum.

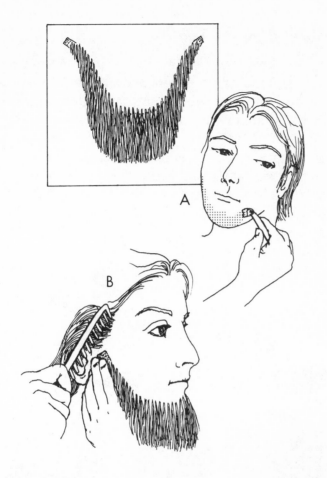

ATTACHING A BEARD

If you cannot rent or buy hairpieces, you can find cheap pieces made of artificial hair in variety stores around Halloween and all year round at theatrical supply houses. These are sometimes too crude for straight realistic makeup, but some are built on starched cambric or even nylon net foundations and can be attached with spirit gum like any professional hairpiece.

To remove a net foundation hairpiece, soften the spirit gum with spirit gum solvent until the piece can be peeled off. Then thoroughly clean the nylon netting with acetone. Clean the face with cold cream or other suitable lotion, then with soap and warm water.

Making beards and mustaches

A simple clip-on clown mustache can be cut from blackened cardboard, as shown, A. That same cardboard or sheet plastic shape can be covered with artificial fur fabric, crepe hair, or even real hair. Of course, the effect will still be broadly comic.

Scraps of real animal fur can be found at thrift shops and cut into beard and mustache shapes. They can be trimmed and even dyed, then secured to the face with spirit gum. A single strip of fur with a length of elastic attached can serve as either clown hair or a farmer's beard, as shown, B.

HOMEMADE HAIRPIECES

TAKING BEARD MEASUREMENTS

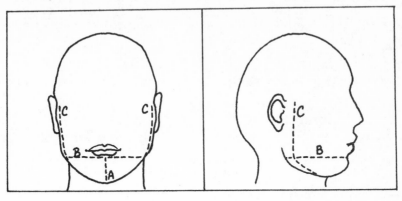

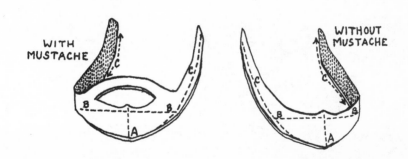

WITH MUSTACHE

WITHOUT MUSTACHE

A crepe beard can also be made on a cambric or nylon base. To get proportions for the individual actress or actor, first measure from the lower lip vertically down the center of the chin and under the beardline, as shown in the illustration, A. Then measure from one back corner of the jawbone around to the crook of the jawbone at the other side, B. Then from the bottom tip of one sideburn, down under the chin and up to the beginning of the other sideburn, C.

Next, use these measurements to lay out the design you want on nylon net, cotton gauze, or cambric. The illustration shows a full beard with mustache and a beard without mustache.

Use straight or push pins to hold this fabric base flat on a board, then glue swatches of crepe hair to the base, "shingling" the hair as you would when building a beard directly on the face, discussed next.

Laying hair directly on the face

A quick and inexpensive white beard or mustache can be made from the lamb's wool sold in variety and drugstores. Using the shingling technique described below, attach the lamb's wool in swatches, using corn syrup and trimming the piece afterward with sharp scissors. Such a beard will hold in place for two or three hours. If the lamb's wool is attached with spirit gum, it should last through one performance.

For a limited number of performances—two to five—it is common practice to build a crepe wool hair beard directly on the face. It can be peeled off after each performance, cleaned and re-used, provided it has been put together and stored carefully. Newly purchased crepe wool must be prepared before it can be used.

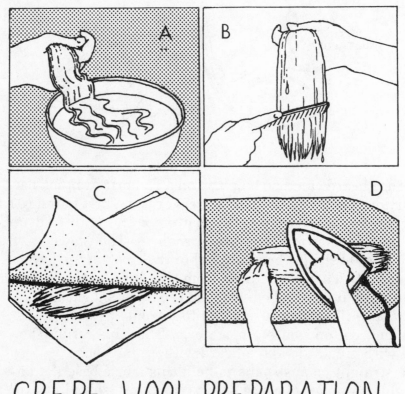

CREPE WOOL PREPARATION

Preparing crepe wool hair

Crepe wool hair is packaged in tight braids and comes in a variety of colors. Solid colors can be used for comic or character makeup—yellow for a local yokel, orange for a clown, black for a comic witch. But for most beards and mustaches, buy the already mixed shades. There are grays of mixed white and black, browns with yellows or reds, blonde colors tempered with strands of brown. If you cannot find the mixed colors, you will have to buy several solid colors and blend them by combing after the wool crepe has been straightened.

To straighten crepe hair, grasp the wrapping string and tug, unraveling a length five to six inches long, then cut. Immerse the swatch in warm water until it begins to lose its curl, A, then remove. Lightly comb the swatch straight and lay it on a fold of paper towel, then place another fold of towel over it, as in the illustration, C. Cut and straighten another swatch and do the same with it, until you have a sufficient stack of flattened or matted swatches. Two or three swatches will do for most mustaches, six to ten for a full beard. To keep the swatches flat while they are drying, weight them down with a heavy object. Once they are dry, they can be straightened further with a dry iron, D. Adjust the iron to its lowest setting, since artificial material changes color if scorched.

Laying a crepe wool mustache

Although a mustache grows down toward the lip, the hairs also tend to slant in each direction outward from the central cleft of the upper lift, toward the outer corners of the mouth. The illustration on page 58 shows the common pattern of mustache and beard growth.

To prepare the crepe hair for your mustache, cut across the grain of the swatch of straightened and dried crepe wool, producing three lengths resembling fringes or very thick eyelashes, 1. The first fringe should be about half an inch long, the second ¾ of an inch, the last an inch or more. Call these the "shingles" of your mustache.

Brush a thin coat of spirit gum on the entire upper lip area to be covered by the mustache and let dry. Next, brush a thinner line of fresh gum just above the top lip line. Grasp the narrowest half-inch fringe and press it to the freshly gummed area above the lip, as in 2.

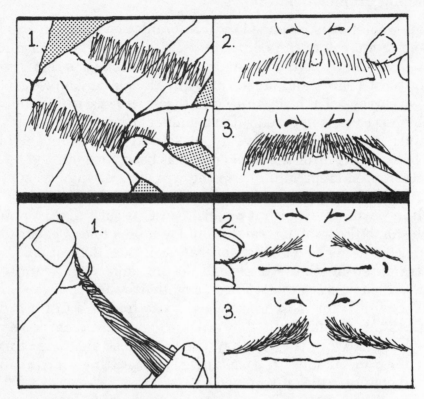

MUSTACHE APPLICATION

Slightly twist the hairs so that they incline outward toward the corners of the lip. Press in place with a damp towel.

When you have laid your first shingle of hair, add more fresh spirit gum above it and apply the second, ¾-inch shingle above, overlapping the top of the first shingle, as in 3. To give the central cleft emphasis, divide the third shingle in two halves, separated by about a quarter to half an inch and press that into place. The three shingles, laying one over the other, give the mustache body in a natural pattern. Lightly comb to blend the hairs and trim to desired style with very sharp mustache or fingernail scissors.

With this basic method you can build a variety of mustaches, from a tiny mustache to one that spreads onto the cheeks and joins the sideburns as muttonchop whiskers.

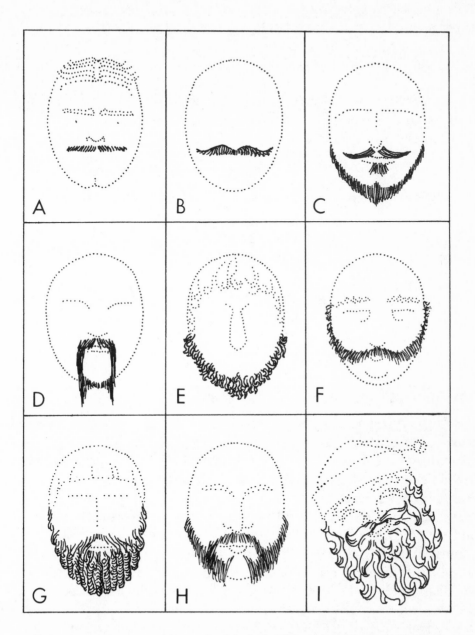

BEARD AND MUSTACHE STYLES

To make a waxed "handlebar" mustache, see the bottom part of the illustration on page 56. Cut a long swatch of two or three inches and divide it into four lengths, applying them horizontally instead of vertically. Twist each length, 1, before you apply it, one on each side. Thicken the mustache by adding the second two lengths, 3. Twist the ends of the finished mustache together with the fingers, or bring to a point with a dab of spirit gum or use real mustache wax.

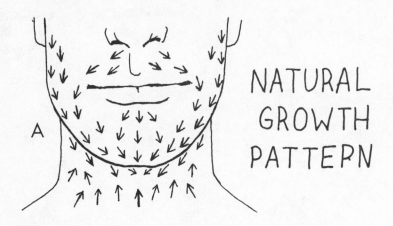

Laying a full beard

Before laying a beard, study the growth pattern of facial hair in the above illustration. The process of laying a crepe hair beard is basically the same as that of a mustache, whether you want a full beard or only a portion of one. It will be helpful to look at the gallery of mustaches and beard types on page 57. Whether you are creating Shakespeare's Vandyke and mustache, C, a Fu Manchu mustache and beard, D, the beard of an ancient Greek, G, Henry VIII's unique pattern of facial hair, H, or the familiar full beard of Santa Claus, I, it is simply a matter of reducing the fundamental full beard pattern to the desired style, or leaving it as full as the style requires.

Clean and dry the face or leave only a very thin film of powdered foundation on the skin. On a piece of paper, draw out a face and the beard style you wish. Keep in mind the natural growth pattern already illustrated. Note that under the chin, the hair grows toward the front; on the sides it grows downward.

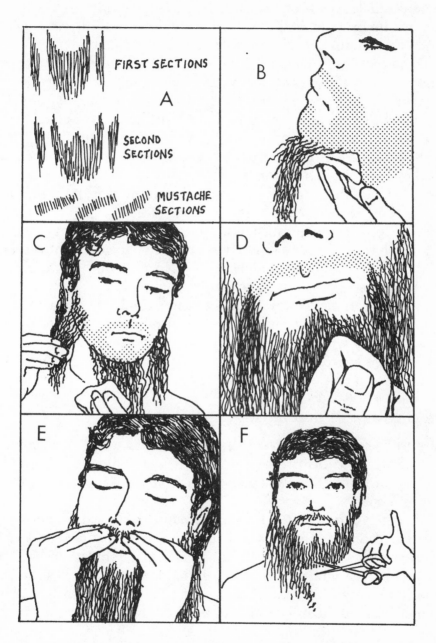

LAYING A FULL BEARD

Divide and trim prepared swatches of crepe hair in the shapes shown on the previous page, A—two sets each of chin and side hair, plus the three fringe lengths needed for the mustache.

Brush spirit gum in a thin layer over the entire area to be covered and allow to dry thoroughly. Start with the area just under the point of the chin, B, first preparing it with a second coat of fresh gum. Then press the chin swatch in place with a damp towel. This first section should thrust forward from under the point of the chin.

Next, gum one side of the jaw and lay one side section in place, then do the same on the other side, C.

Next, add fresh gum for the second pair of side hair swatches, tapering their roots at each outside corner of the mouth, as shown, D.

Finally, apply more gum; then flatten and shape the final swatch of chin hair so that it peaks slightly up toward the center of the lower lip and press it into place as shown in D. Now lay in the mustache, E, following the directions in the previous section of this chapter.

Allow all sections to dry in place, then comb with your fingers, gently blending the sections together and removing any loose hairs. Trim and shape with sharp scissors, F.

The stubble beard of a man who hasn't shaved is produced with ¼-inch snippets of crepe wool pressed onto a thin film of spirit gum.

Removing beards and mustaches

Careful use of spirit gum solvent in removing a beard or mustache will preserve the hairpiece for future use. The piece should be powdered on the back to prevent folds from sticking together, then stored in a box.

While spirit gum gives a firmer grip on the skin, a hairpiece will last longer if liquid latex is used instead of gum. Liquid latex comes in white and flesh colors, the flesh being best for this purpose. Apply the latex just as you would spirit gum, but build up two or three foundation layers before affixing the crepe hair. And, as you add each swatch of hair, delicately dab latex in under the roots to further imbed it in the foundation or nylon base. Latex dries very fast, so you must work quickly but carefully, doing only small sections at a time.

Such a hairpiece can be easily peeled off after performance, its inner surface powdered, and the piece stored.

6
Character Makeup

Because the impulse to transform oneself is common to all actors, many find character acting the most satisfying and character makeup the most challenging. Character makeup can produce a simple aging of your basic look, or it can transform you into an entirely different person, perhaps of another race or time. To a degree, makeup can give an audience an immediate indication of character before the actor speaks a line.

Physiognomy

This word refers to the old-fashioned study of faces in relation to character. Once considered a science, physiognomy is now treated, at best, as interesting speculation.

Obviously, the shape of the face, the contours of the skull, the size of the nose, and the color of the skin are not reliable indications of a person's strengths and weaknesses, temperament or character.

On the other hand, audiences have deeply ingrained opinions about faces, and they are not inclined to see someone with lips loosely open and a receding chin as strong-willed; or a character with a scarred cheek, tattoos, and bad teeth as reliable. Furthermore, there is some merit in the theory that one's experiences and attitudes become written on one's face. It could be fairly argued that Scrooge's cynical view of life and penny-pinching habits contributed to the usual picture of the Christmas miser as having a pinched brow and sour, downturned mouth.

How broadly or how subtly the common interpretations of facial characteristics are used in creating theatrical makeup depends on the script and the taste and judgment of the director and individual actor.

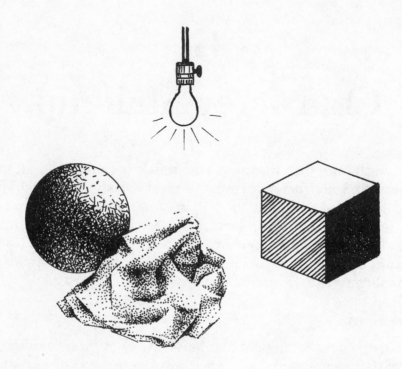

Light and shadow

In Chapter 3 we discussed the optical illusions achieved by horizontal and vertical emphasis and juxtaposition of light and dark. Keep those principles in mind as you consider reshaping the face with light and shade, which is essential for effective character makeup.

The contours of the skull produce the fundamental prominences and depressions on your face that catch the light by varying degrees, leaving highlights and shadows. The sharper prominences such as cheekbones produce more hard-edged shadows like those on the cube in the illustration above. The addition of pouchy flesh, particularly in the older or plumper face, produces softer-edged blending of light and dark, as with the drapery in the drawing.

The drapery and sphere indicate the subtler and more complex blending of hard and soft-edged shadowing typical of the human face.

Reshaping with light and shadow

To use makeup paint and color to alter an individual face, you must take into account the basic shadow and light pattern you are given in bone and flesh. You cannot completely transform the basic sculpting of a face, but you can alter the emphasis in selected areas and add details such as wrinkles and blemishes, using lining color.

Hollow cheeks

Hunger, old age, illness and even emotional tension tend to deepen the hollows in the face and make the bonier areas seem more prominent. To create the appearance of hollow cheeks, first apply your foundation, then suck in your cheeks to locate the natural hollows in your face. Brush a dark shading color in a rough Y shape under each cheekbone, as shown for one side only in A. Blend this "hollow" into the foundation with your finger or a sponge. The upper edge of the hollow along the cheekbone should be blended to form a harder edge; that is, the demarcation between the foundation color and the shading color should be relatively narrow and abrupt. The

SHADOW
AND
MAKEUP

area where the hollow fades downward into cheek and jaw should have a softer edge: the shadow color should blend into the foundation color more gradually.

You can further emphasize the hard-edged shadow where the hollow is deepest under the ridge of the cheekbone. Keep in mind that light against dark makes the dark seem darker. Select a shading color lighter than your foundation and apply it in a crescent pattern along the upper portion of the cheekbone, B. Blend this highlight more sharply along the edge of the bone, less sharply up into the eye area.

You have done your first facial sculpting with shadow and highlight. Highlight on the bony prominences, shadow in the deeper hollows.

Rouge can also be used to change the contour of actors' cheeks. A touch of bluish rouge down the side of the cheek gives a drawn or sickly look. Bright rouge below the cheekbone gives an effect of healthy plumpness. Dark rouge has the same effect as shadowing; blend it downward from under the cheekbone for a hollow-cheeked look.

Other features can be emphasized or exaggerated by use of shadow and highlight. Darkening the natural indentations on either side of the brow gives an impression of gauntness, illness, aging, or tension. The nose can be sharpened or narrowed by darkening the natural shadows at either side and in the frown furrows of the brow, then highlighting the bridge of the nose, the tops of the nostrils, and the tops of the brow furrows.

You can even use light and shadow technique to create a broken nose, as described in our Gallery chart for pirate makeup.

The nasolabial folds

Of all the facial creases and folds that indicate age or state of mind, the two clefts running from the side of the nose down either side of the mouth are the most expressive. These nasolabial folds, in C of the illustration, can be deepened with shadow and highlight, or minimized by filling them in with lighter rather than darker shading. They can even be altered subtly with light and shade to give the appearance of a smile to an otherwise naturally solemn expression.

RESCULPTING THE EYES

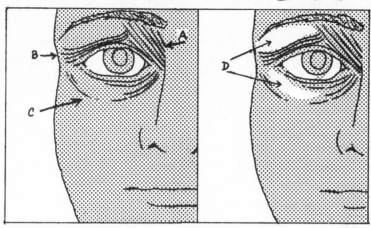

Eyes

Resculpting the eyes with light and shadow requires attention to prominences and depressions already on your face. Squinting into the mirror will indicate certain features of the eye more clearly, such as the laugh wrinkles at the outer corners, the way the lids draw back when you widen your eyes. The deeper the shading and the brighter the highlights used in the illustrations above, the greater the effect of aging, illness, or gauntness.

Study the illustration and the areas as indicated by letter.

A: Shade the long triangle from the inner corner of the eye down toward the bridge of the nose. The blending edge should be sharper against the nose and have a softer edge as it blends outward into the crease above the eyelid.

B: Draw a soft line of shadow along the eyelid crease, extending it downward to the corner of the eye, with a slight lift at the end into the outer eye creases. Emphasis of this kind can give a look of sadness as well as age.

C: It is the hollow of softer flesh along the edge of the eye socket that creates bags under the eyes. Shadow the hollow, giving it a softer lower edge as it blends outward toward the side of the face and corner of the eye.

D: Finally, add the highlights in a shade lighter than your foundation, then powder.

For additional emphasis on the bulging undereye pouches, simply use deeper shadows and brighter highlights.

As you noticed when you squinted into the mirror, there are myriad smaller lines and creases within the overall light and shadow pattern. These are indicated in makeup with what is called lining.

Highlighting

But before the lining is applied, you must complete your light and shadow work by highlighting the prominences of the face you are creating. Highlights are accomplished with makeup of a hue identical or similar to your foundation color, but higher in value, that is, lighter because it has more white in it. (Hollows are emphasized with a shade lower in value than the foundation, that is, with more black in it.)

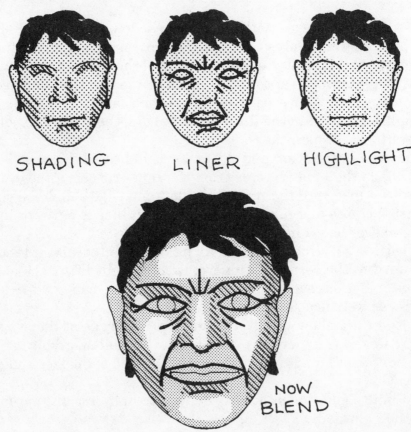

SHADING   LINER   HIGHLIGHT

NOW BLEND

Apply the major highlights with your finger or a brush. The common major highlights are where natural prominences occur: the cheekbones, the brow, the bridge of the nose, the tip of the chin. Blend them into the foundation at their edges, creating harder edges where the hollow is deepest, softer edges where it stands out more sharply from the face, softer where it slopes more smoothly to the facial surface. In the face illustrated, you see rudimentary patterns for shadows, highlights, and basic lining.

Lining

The finer lines of the face can be applied over the completed overall light and shadow sculpting. Squinting and otherwise altering your expression in the mirror will show you how the skin wrinkles in old age, illness, or under tension. Some hollows deepen, some prominences seem more evident, and lines appear, usually between hollows and prominences.

A dour person is more likely to have deeply cut nasolabial folds that pull the corners of the mouth downward. A melancholy person is likely to develop furrows across the forehead. An intense person is likely to develop deep vertical grooves between the eyebrows from continual frowning.

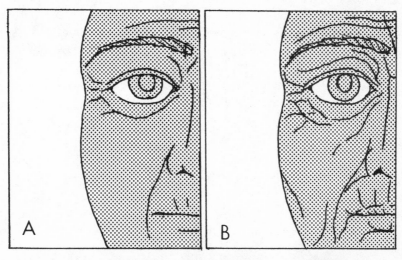

CREATING FACIAL LINES

The illustration shows the most common patterns: A, the basic pattern, B, the lines multiplied and deepened in old age. Such lines are added in liner color over the light and shadow sculpting. You can apply the paint with one of the pointed paper pencils called stomps, twirling it in the makeup and then applying it in light, smooth strokes, twirling the stomp between your fingers as you draw. Liner color can also be applied with a finely pointed brush, but the easiest tool to use is an eyebrow pencil—medium or light brown.

You can give the lines realistic depth by first drawing in white or light-colored highlight, usually a brown, then use a shade a touch darker than your shadow color to draw a line exactly parallel to the lighter one and snugly against it. The finer the lines, the tighter together they should be. Try to taper them, just as the lines on your skin are mostly deeper and thicker at the center, more shallow and finer at the ends.

Blend carefully with the tip of your little finger, the stomp, or a brush, but leave light and shadow still distinct. Don't blend the lighter and darker lines so thoroughly that you muddy the line.

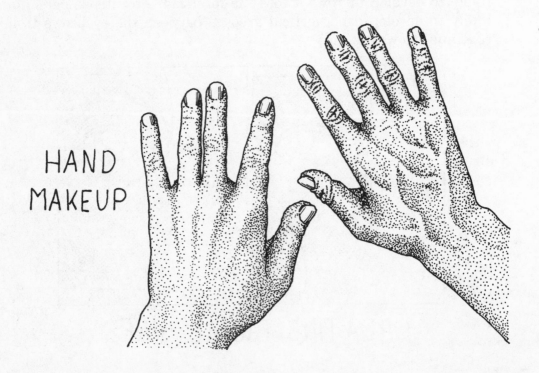

HAND
MAKEUP

Hands

Hands also indicate state of health and age. From middle to old age the bones become more noticeable, and wrinkles increase in depth and number. Sculpt the hands as you did the face, first applying foundation, if needed, then highlighting, then shadowing, then lining. Highlight the finger bones and shadow them to either side. To emphasize the knuckles, first make a fist and circle each knuckle with shadow, then splay the fingers on a table top and press down, so the creases across the knuckles are exaggerated. With your forefinger spread a thin film of highlight color over the creases. Then blend all light and shadow edges with a brush. To emphasize the veins on the backs of the hands, shadow and highlight the natural veins and blend.

Old age makeup

This is mostly an extension of the shadow, highlight and lining pattern already discussed, with a few special notes. The foundation is paler, the shadows deeper, the highlights sharper. To paint the complex folds and wrinkles in the neck, tuck your chin in and locate the natural lines, then shadow and highlight them.

To simulate broken veins on the cheeks and on the side of the nose and nostrils, rub a coarse sponge over dark red cake makeup or eye shadow, then dab lightly over the area. If this stippling effect proves to be too coarse and obvious, you can mute it with additional powder or foundation.

To age the mouth, extend the foundation over the natural lip outline, muting the natural pinkness and narrowing the lips. To make the lips even more sunken, paint a thin, dark lip shape inside the natural outline. Shadow and highlight can emphasize the deep sag of the muscles at either side of the mouth. For extreme old age, use dark liner and highlight to create the vertical seams on the lips.

You can add to the reddened impression of old eyes with a thin red line painted on the bottom of the eyelid. Doing the same along the line of the top lid adds an even more sickly look.

Eyebrows and lashes can be aged by the addition of white shadow or professional hair whitener, using the applicator supplied or with a makeup brush. Stroke in the natural direction of the hairs. Do not plaster the hairs into a solid white mass.

Constructions

Sometimes paint is not enough to change the texture of the skin and enlarge or alter facial features like the nose and eyes. Particularly in character makeup, features are frequently built up by application of ready-made materials such as nose putty or mortician's wax. These makeup constructions or artificial parts may be glued in place, using makeup to conceal the joining to the skin.

Nose putty

Nose putty is used to build up noses as well as other features—chins, ears, etc.—that have a firm, bony base and little mobility. Using nose putty takes skill, so it is best to practice before any rehearsal or performance.

The putty becomes softer and more pliable as it is worked with warm fingers. Mixing the putty with a small amount of grease paint or cold cream, worked in with the fingers, will increase its pliability. But be cautious, for too much pliability under hot lights during performance may make your false nose ooze right down your face!

Including a little spirit gum in the mixture will help it stick and counteract the loosening effects of perspiration. You can also mix in greasepaint to bring the putty's color closer to that of your foundation.

Before applying putty, clean the area of moisture and grease with a dry tissue or a cotton ball dipped into a little astringent. Some actors prefer to apply a thin film of spirit gum before adding the putty.

Pinch a small piece from the stick of putty and knead it until it is pliable. Non-greasy hairdressing on the finger tips can prevent it from sticking to the fingers, but remember that any such addition to the putty itself can make it too soft. Apply the wad of putty to the area, pinching and molding it until you have the rough shape you are after, A. Next press it down at the sides to seal it to the skin and sculpt it to shape, B.

APPLYING NOSE PUTTY

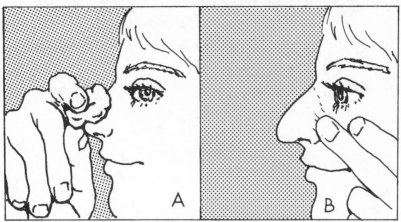

When you have the shape you want, match its color to your makeup color by stippling foundation on with a sponge, dabbing gently rather than rubbing. Some smoothing with the finger is still possible. For a nose with broken veins, stipple lightly with a red shadow makeup before powdering.

To remove a construction of nose putty, grasp the shape with finger and thumb and gently rock until it comes loose. It can be rolled into a ball and stored for two or three more uses, provided you haven't worked too much makeup or spirit gum into it.

Mortician's wax

Mortician's wax, commercially known as Derma-wax, is easier to sculpt into shape than nose putty, but it is also more easily loosened by facial movement. For this reason, putty is usually used in stage productions, when makeup must sometimes hold in place for an hour or more. But because wax is translucent, it holds up better under close-ups for film, video, and photography.

Mix in dark cream-stick foundation to bring the wax to a color match with your foundation, mixing it on a plastic or glass sheet with a palette knife rather than your fingers.

Before applying wax, coat the area with spirit gum, C. Then press a thin coating of cotton wool fibers into the gum to create an adhesive base for the wax.

APPLYING MORTICIAN'S WAX

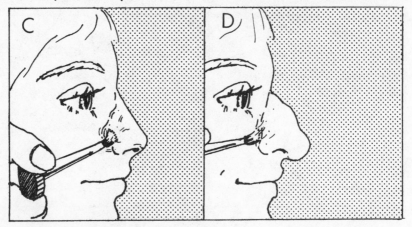

Next, press a wad of wax in place, build and sculpt the shape as you would with nose putty, but work with fingers dipped in cold water, not cream. If necessary, press on extra small balls of wax to make the shape larger. You can also work wax with a spoon or spatula dipped in water.

Finally, the whole built-up feature must be coated, D, with a special sealer available from theatrical suppliers. Mortician's wax is also useful for special applications such as scars and wounds, described later.

Constructions and artificial features can also be built up directly on the skin with liquid latex. But latex is best used for the making of removable and reusable prosthetic parts.

Prostheses

Prosthetics is a medical term meaning the fitting of artificial parts to the body or face. Such ready-made three-dimensional false pieces, usually made of latex rubber, can be found at theatrical supply houses. More crudely formed prosthetic pieces are included in the makeup kits sold around Halloween. The most obvious make-up use of a prosthesis is the clown's big red nose, which can be fabricated from a rubber ball and elastic, as illustrated in the final chapter.

You can also cut noses and other features from latex rubber Halloween masks and use them as prosthetic parts of a particular character makeup. False noses and other prosthetic features can also be made cheaply from papier-mâché.

Ready-made theatrical prosthetic pieces are attached to the face or body with spirit gum, E, F, the edges of the piece pressed into the tacky gum with a damp towel, or, in narrow areas beside the nose, with an orange stick. Since regular greasepaint eats into the latex, the piece must be colored with a special rubber-mask greasepaint. Cheaper coloring, like cream-based stick makeup, is safe if it is mixed with a little castor oil. The makeup should be blended well where the piece joins the foundation. Stippling with a darker foundation shade or with rouge gives a texture which helps conceal the edge where the piece joins the skin. Powder to blend further.

Carefully remove the piece so you can reuse it. If you try to pull it directly off the skin, it will tear along the edges. Instead, dip a brush into spirit gum remover and work it gently up between the edge of the piece and the skin, then lift the piece off bit by bit as the gum seal dissolves.

Powder the piece on the inside to prevent surfaces from sticking together. A carefully removed and powdered prosthetic piece can be reused up to ten times.

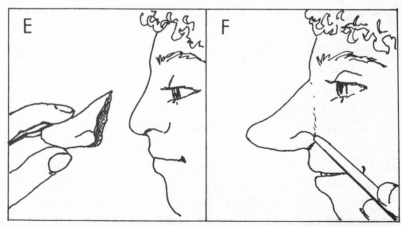

ATTACHING A PROSTHESIS

Casting latex parts

You can make your own prosthetic parts from liquid latex. The complex and fabulous makeups you have seen in such movies as *Planet of the Apes* require a life mask of the actor cast in plaster of Paris. The prosthesis segments—nose, wrinkled brow, hairy cheeks—are then built up on the plaster mask with combinations of latex, crepe hair and even bread crumbs for a coarse complexion. Directions for making a life mask can be found in various makeup books in your library.

However, the process of designing, casting and curing professional latex prostheses is too complex and demanding for this book. Details of the procedure vary with the different types and brands of latex. Supply houses and manufacturers offer complete directions on mixing, casting, and curing.

There is a simpler way to produce acceptable latex parts, particularly noses, pointed ears, and bulging foreheads. You can first model an approximation of the natural feature, such as your own nose, in modeling clay (one brand name, Plasticene) and then paint on layers of liquid latex, which are allowed to dry before they are removed from the clay.

To produce the several lengths of nose to be applied each time Pinocchio tells a lie, first sculpt your own cheeks and nose in modeling clay. The closer you can come to the correct dimensions and modeling of your natural nose, the better will be the fit of the finished piece.

Next, coat the clay model with a thin film of petroleum jelly. This will make it possible to peel the latex piece off once it is finished.

Using flesh-colored, air-drying liquid latex, brush on five to eight layers of liquid, allowing each layer to dry before applying the next. In the case of Pinocchio, extend the end of the nose with lengths of cork or sewing thimbles, applying additional layers of latex over them. To add texture or blemishes—the wart on a witch's nose, for example—sprinkle bread crumbs on the first layers, then cover with further layers, or place a piece of puffed rice or a round wad of cotton on the first layers to make the wart, then cover with further layers.

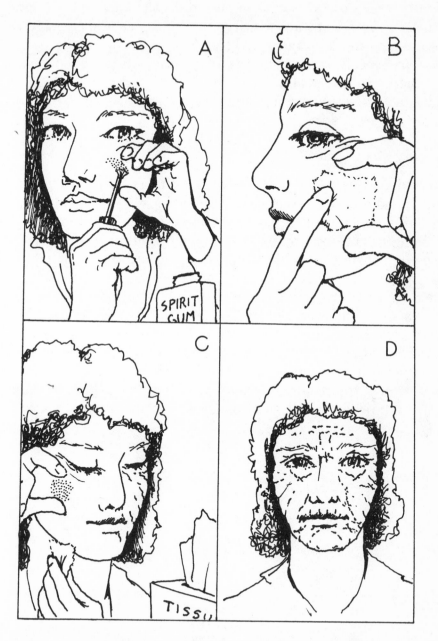

WRINKLING THE SKIN

Finally, the prosthesis can be peeled off the clay piece, allowed to dry further, then be attached with spirit gum, as described above.

To make pointed ears or a bulging forehead, first model your own ear or forehead in modeling clay, then build up the effect you want with successive layers of latex.

Manufacturers also provide a latex that can be dried in a household oven for a more lasting, reusable prosthesis.

Wrinkled skin

For stage work, shadow and highlight sculpting with paint is usually adequate to give the skin an aged look. Film or video close-up work can benefit from three-dimensional wrinkling and it is useful for the more grotesque monster makeups popular on Halloween.

Here is a basic method for wrinkling the skin using spirit gum or latex and facial cleansing tissue. (It is not a good idea to use this method on sensitive skin or skin with fine facial hair.)

Take a single thickness of tissue and cut it into sections about 3×3 inches. Use your finger and thumb to stretch a 3×3 inch area of the skin taut and flat, then brush on a thin layer of spirit gum or latex, A. As this grows tacky, and with the skin still held taut and flat, press on a section of the tissue, B. Apply a second coat of gum or latex and dry with a hair dryer, still holding the skin taut. When the laminated

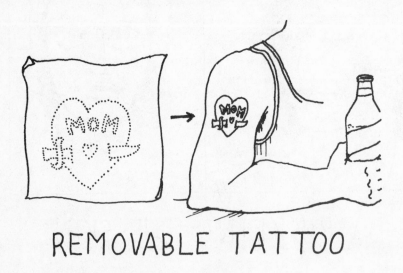

REMOVABLE TATTOO

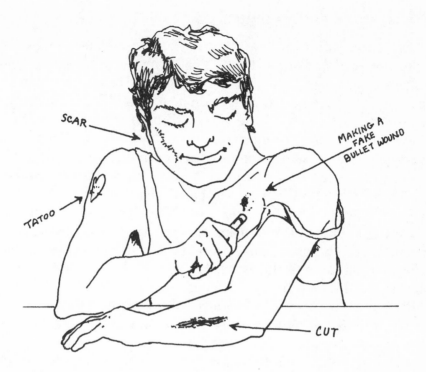

gum and tissue are thoroughly dry, release the skin, allowing it to draw into wrinkles.

Repeat, working section by section and overlapping tissue slightly at the join between areas. That done, make up with suitable foundation, stippling with shadow or rouge for texture and highlight, D. You can emphasize these artificial wrinkles by brushing on liner color, darkening the crevices and adding fine highlights across the top of each wrinkle.

After performance, this latex-wrinkled skin appliqué can be peeled right off. If spirit gum is used, however, spirit gum solvent will have to be used to soften the piece until it can be peeled away.

Liquid collodion is also used to create scars and wrinkles, the collodion applied directly to the skin. It dries and tightens the skin, pulling it into wrinkles. But never use collodion on any area larger than 1×3 inches. Frequent use of collodion can damage the skin.

After removing latex or gum wrinkle appliqué, clean the skin with soap and warm water, dry, and treat with a good skin toning cream or lotion.

Tattoos, scars, and wounds

Design the tattoo first on paper, then trace the outline with pin pricks close together and through the paper. Put this paper template in place on the skin and pat black or dark brown powder onto the paper so it will come through on the skin. The resultant dotted outline will then serve as a guide. Finish the tattoo with colored eyebrow pencils or cake makeup applied with a fine brush.

The quickest scars are made with non-flexible collodion, available in some drugstores and through pharmaceutical supply houses as well as most makeup suppliers. Paint the scar area with the collodion. As it dries it will pucker the skin. Then use makeup to highlight and shadow the indentations. Do not use this method on the same area of the skin more than half a dozen times, or you risk permanent damage to the skin. Latex scars can be made by sculpting them first in tacky latex on a smooth surface, such as a small mirror or sheet of glass. Mix in colored powder or tiny scrapings from cake makeup to add color: blues, reds, even a touch of green at appropriate spots within the scar. Allow the latex scar to dry, peel off the glass, and stick in place on the skin with spirit gum. Touch up with additional makeup color and blend edges with foundation makeup.

Makeup suppliers offer ready-made latex wounds of every grisly variety, and cheap appliqué wounds are available around Halloween. You can make your own wounds with mortician's wax. First prepare the area with a thin coat of spirit gum; then use a spatula to spread the wax and sculpt it. Color as you see fit with lining color or cake makeup and a brush, darker red and bluish in the depth of the wound, lighter along the edges. Powder lightly, then squeeze red liquid makeup or professional stage blood into the cut with an eyedropper. Fix it all in place with a thin film of spirit gum or other fixative.

A bullet wound can be simulated with the same wax base and the blunt end of a pencil pressed into the wax circle to indicate the hole where the bullet went in. Line the hole with black and red, seal, and add a dribble of stage blood or vermillion makeup.

7
Makeup Gallery

Here is a chance to apply previously discussed makeup methods and principles to specific makeup projects. Some of the exercises in our gallery are for generic types, some for specific theatrical and literary characters. In each case, the colors are given for foundation, highlights, shadow, and cheek, lip, and eye makeup. Most gallery patterns can be used, in part or in whole, for other, similar characters, as noted under each heading.

The gallery is not meant to be a complete listing of theatrical types or characters, but it does cover virtually all the makeup challenges the young actor will confront—and the techniques needed to meet those challenges.

Makeup for the gallery characters that follow ranges from the simple to the elaborate. For example, actors playing Robin Hood, Cinderella, Queen Guinevere, and Sir Lancelot all wear relatively simple makeup as compared to Doctor Fu Manchu, Cyrano de Bergerac, Cleopatra, or Pocahontas. Actors transforming themselves to look like a vampire, a clown, a space alien, or the Cowardly Lion from *The Wizard of Oz,* will be even more challenged. Keep in mind that the basics of highlighting and shading are applied to the makeup of Snow White and Frankenstein's monster alike.

Above all, young actors should have fun creating these characters. Using basic techniques, they will find that in every actor lies a makeup artist.

YOUNG HEROES

Characters:	Sir Lancelot, Robin Hood, Allan-a-Dale, any young hero (called juveniles in theatre)
Foundation:	Light, deep, or warm tan
Highlights:	Pale or ivory
Shading:	Warm tan or deep brown
Lips and cheeks:	Lips medium red or lake; rouge medium red
Eyes:	Dark brown liner and eyebrow pencil, dark brown or gray eye shadow

Makeup notes

All of the above paints should be used sparingly. When possible, match makeup to the actor's original coloring. For instance, the actor shown as Allan-a-Dale in the illustration, B, is blonde, as the character is most often described, so his makeup should simply strengthen his natural coloring to keep the face from being faded out by stage lights. In the case of Robin Hood, A, a light complexion was strengthened with tan foundation and light eyeshadow used to brighten rather flat eyesockets.

Apply foundation as thinly as possible, but strong enough not to fade under lights. Keep eye makeup to a minimum. Naturally well-formed lips should be left without any makeup, as the smallest amount of lip color can give a lipsticked appearance. Rouge should usually be applied only to sculpt the cheeks and only secondarily to add color. When eyebrows need to be strengthened, use only light pencil strokes in the direction of the natural growth.

For a prince's mustache or goatee, see Chapter 5.

YOUNG HEROINES

Characters:	Cinderella, Snow White, Maid Marian, Helen of Troy, Betsy Ross, Miss Liberty
Foundation:	Peach, creamy, or light tan
Highlights:	Lighter than foundation: pale peach, pale creamy, pale tan
Shading:	Warm light brown
Lips and cheeks:	Light or medium red lipstick and rouge
Eyes:	For a natural look, neutral gray or brown eye shadow, or color harmonizing with costume; light to dark brown eyebrow pencil and eye liner

Makeup notes

Follow instructions in Chapter 2 for straight makeup. Where corrective highlights and shading are needed, either to adjust the actor's appearance or to add character, consult Chapter 3. The order of application described in those chapters should be followed: first block eyebrows if necessary, then apply foundation evenly, make up eyes and eyebrows, add any highlighting and shading, then lips, and finally add rouge and lip gloss if necessary.

Just as every actress is different, so every princess-like character varies from the so-called norm. Since the Maid Marian shown in the illustration is a blonde and light-skinned, a creamy peach is used for the foundation and pale shading with neutral eye shadow to retain the delicate look, only strengthening it overall so it will not fade under stage lights. The Snow White illustrated follows a Disney design that has become traditional, but you may want to vary it, depending on the qualities of the actress and your interpretation of the character.

The first purposes are to improve natural facial qualities, to make adjustments suitable to the character portrayed, and to strengthen the desired impression under theatrical light.

QUEENS

Characters:	Queen of Hearts, Queen Guinevere, Mary Queen of Scots
Foundation:	Peach or pink mixed with small amount of ivory
Highlights:	Ivory
Shading:	Deep brown or lake
Lips and cheeks:	Dark or medium red lipstick, medium red or bright red rouge
Eyes:	Brown eyebrow pencil, brown eye liner, brown mascara, blue-grey, dark mauve, or dark green eye shadow

Makeup notes

This is middle age to early old age makeup—the so-called mature years of most queens and other women of character and position. The makeup is distinguished by at least some light and shadow sculpting for character, as described in Chapters 3 and 6. Degree of application depends on the age of the queen, but if the actress still has the brighter bloom of youth, the foundation should have more ivory content to indicate the more sallow coloring of the older woman.

Some lining will also be called for around the eyes and mouth, and the mauve and gray-blue eye shadow colors add to the impression of aging eye sockets. Using a darker red on the upper lip than the lower adds to the effect.

The Queen of Hearts makeup shown in the illustration, A, uses light and shade for more angular sculpting of the face, with wrinkles and facial folds added in brown liner with parallel, very thin yellow highlight. This particular queen sports a small heart on one cheek which can be red or black. The makeup for Queen Guinevere, B, suggests maturity, but is softer and not as angular as that of the Queen of Hearts.

Characters:	King Arthur, King Richard the Lion-Hearted, King of Hearts
Foundation:	Light tan mixed with florid or pink; creamy or sallow for ill-health
Highlights:	Ivory
Shading:	Pale brown or lake; olive brown for ill-health
Lips and cheeks:	Pale pink rouge, medium red or lake for lips
Eyes:	Dark brown eyebrow pencil, brown liner, brown or lake eye shadow

Makeup notes

A man's appearance in middle age varies according to his health and lifestyle. King Richard the Lion-Hearted is often depicted as relatively young, as shown, A. King Arthur is usually somewhat older, his hair could be frosted with liquid white. The chubby King of Hearts shown here, B, has a face sculpted in highlight and shading to simulate the deeper folds and sagging jowls of a fleshy middle age. Study instructions in Chapters 3 and 6 for makeup selection and application methods. For wigs and beards, see Chapters 4 and 5.

BLACKS

A

B

Characters:	Othello, Frederick Douglass, Sojourner Truth, Harriet Tubman, Martin Luther King, Jr., Rosa Parks
Foundation:	Dark brown or blue-black cake makeup
Highlights:	Light beige or brown transparent liquid makeup
Shading:	Black or dark brown cake makeup
Lips and cheeks:	Deep, strong red
Eyes:	Dark brown or black kohl pencil eye liner

Makeup notes

For a white actor playing a dark-skinned or black person, the idea is to darken the natural features while at the same time giving the skin the lustrous highlights of a naturally dark or black skin.

There are assorted tones of dark makeup available in hard and soft greasepaint and cream sticks. But any suitable shade of cake makeup will do as well. Apply this dark makeup with a sponge dipped—not in water as usual—but in a translucent liquid makeup of a lighter tone. Such translucent makeups are available at some cosmetics counters and at theatrical supply houses.

Sponge carefully to give a smooth blend. Allow to dry. For highlight areas such as cheekbones, nose ridge and point of chin, moisten a second sponge with the liquid highlight only. Now rub the highlights with this sponge, letting the darker foundation gleam through where it stretches over bone. Add shadows of black cake makeup, smoothly blended at the edges. Do not use white around the eyes, but line them with dark brown or black kohl. Lacking that, use a black eye liner or eyebrow pencil. This basic makeup is suitable for such characters as Shakespeare's Othello, A.

Elderly black men and women usually have cottony white hair. Use a wig or whiten curly hair with hair whitener. Abolitionist Frederick Douglass, B, had salt and pepper hair. It can be suggested by laborious white streaking of naturally curly hair, or with a suitable wig.

ASIAN FEMALE

A

B

Characters:	Geisha, women in *The Mikado*
Foundation:	Ivory with yellow or peach for Chinese
	Ivory with peach or olive for Japanese
Highlights:	Ivory or white
Shading:	Olive-brown
Lips and cheeks:	Light or medium red
Eyes:	Black eye liner, white highlights

Makeup notes

Never use pure yellow or flat white foundation except for stylized and comic makeups such as those in *The Mikado,* and even in that play, ivory with peach or yellow is best for the straight parts.

The eyelid shape typical of the Chinese and Japanese is known as the epicanthic or Mongolian fold. It does not tilt the actual eyes as is commonly believed. The eyes remain horizontal and are not slits but almond-shaped. The fold does curve downward over the inside corner of the eye and the eyebrow is cut shorter at the top of its arch, seeming to give a lift to the eye, A.

The Mongolian fold can be simulated with makeup. (For Asian eyes with artificial lids, see ahead, Asian Male.) To begin, block out the outside ends of the eyebrows with soap (see Chapter 3). Next, apply the foundation and light and shadow modeling.

Now set to work on the eyes. Highlight the bony bulge above the outer upper eyelid with white, blending it up onto the blocked-out end of the eyebrow. Blend edges of this whitened area into the foundation for each eye. With an eyebrow pencil, sketch in the shortened eyebrows. Outline the eye with eye liner as shown, using a brush to draw a fine black line along the edge of the top lid, extending it slightly downward at the outer corner, then up again. This gives the outer corners of the eyes a wing-like effect. At the inner corner of each eye, curve the line of black over the edge and in toward the nose, simulating the downward fold.

For the long, more aquiline face of the northern Chinese or the Mandarin, use light and shadow under the cheekbones and on the nose. A Caucasian nose can be broadened and shortened using highlight to de-emphasize the natural nose bridge, plus extra shadowing straight across the bottom of the nose tip and bottoms of the nostrils.

For the geisha look B, use lipstick or paint to exaggerate the lips into a rosebud shape, then highlight the center of the lower lip to make it seem fuller. Don't forget to make up the hands and other exposed skin to match your foundation.

Hair can be coiffed as shown or a wig may be worn. False fingernails emphasize the slim hand of an upper class Asian woman. For an aged Asian woman, use the same foundation, shading and eye makeup, but apply the wrinkling and aging extras described in Chapter 6.

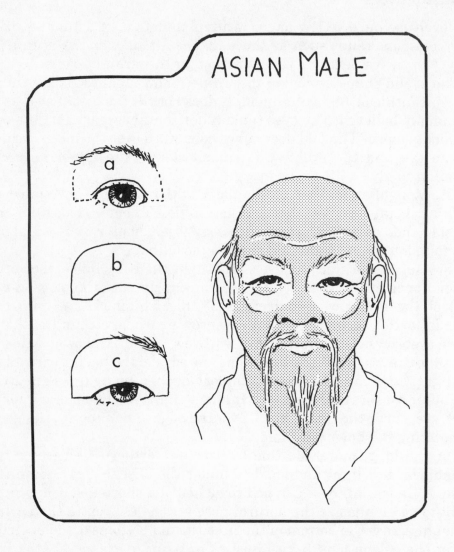

ASIAN MALE

Characters:	Characters in *The Mikado,* such elderly Mandarins as Doctor Fu Manchu
Foundation:	Ivory mixed with olive, tan, or yellow
Highlights:	White or ivory
Shading:	Olive-brown
Lips and cheeks:	Medium-red
Eyes:	Black eye liner, white for highlights

Makeup notes

The illustration shows an elderly man, but the same foundation, highlight and shading colors apply to a younger man, as do the false eyelids.

You can cut false lids from wide surgical tape or fine chamois leather: a, shows the area to be covered by the tape. Cut out the shape, b, and attach it as shown, c. The tape will stick by itself; the chamois must be attached with spirit gum. But first, line the inside of the false lid with a small crescent of paper positioned where the patch will touch your natural eyelid. Do *not* stick the patch to your eyelid, but attach it to the brow and outside corners of the eye socket, leaving the natural lid free to move.

The patch should cover the outer third of the eyebrow at the top. If it does not, block the ends of the eyebrows with soap or white cake, as for the Asian Female. Use tweezers to lift a few eyebrow hairs out from under the patch and let them fall over to help conceal the upper edge of the false lid.

Make up the false lid with foundation color first, then highlight it, applying white to the bulge. For a young man, outline the eyes only lightly. For a more stylized or comic effect, as for some of the characters in *The Mikado,* you can use eye liner to add the short downward droop of the Mongolian fold at the inner corner and add the wing-like upward lift at the outside corner. Japanese *Noh* plays use such dramatically stylized, even bizarre extensions of the basic Asian male makeup.

The Asian man's nose can be flattened and shortened with highlight and shadow; see Asian Female. Shading on the cheeks at an oblique angle toward the corners of the mouth gives a bonier look. Lips must not be as bright as those of the female, but highlight should be used on the lower lip to make it fuller.

For the aging Asian male, use yellow with ivory foundation for a paler, sallow skin tone. Use the color groups given above when you follow earlier directions for aging and wrinkling. The wispy white mustache and goatee can be built on the face with spirit gum and crepe wool (see Chapter 5).

Characters:	South Americans of European descent (Simon Bolívar, Evita Perón, Benito Pablo Juárez, Emiliano Zapata); Mediterraneans (Don Quixote, Zorba); *commedia dell'arte* (Pantalone, Il Dottore)
Foundation:	Dark golden-tan or golden olive
Highlights:	Golden-olive, lighter than foundation
Shading:	Golden-olive, darker than foundation
Lips and cheeks:	Women: dark red rouge, mouth outlined with dark red lip pencil; Men: less color
Eyes:	Strong, dark eyebrows, plenty of mascara, black or dark brown eyebrow pencil

Makeup notes

Mediterraneans and their South American descendants usually have strong bone structure, a full mouth, and large eyes. Apply foundation, then highlight the nose bridge, chin, and cheekbones, sculpting with light and shadow. If your eyebrows are light, strengthen them with eyebrow pencil, emphasizing a high arch. Use a strong eye shadow on the eyelids. For glamour, B, you can enlarge the eyes with black eye liner, giving them a fish-tail shape, highlighting the boniness beneath the outer end of the eyebrow.

Outline the mouth with a dark red pencil to make it larger, fill in with red lipstick or cake, then add a touch of gloss to the lower lip for fullness.

Latin males should be made up with less vivid eye shadow, but mascara can be used to give a dark-eyed look.

Some Latin American types do not have bony facial structure, but a broader, rounder look, often the result of a blending with Indian blood. For a Mexican bandito, for example, or a native revolutionary like Emiliano Zapata, A, the nose can be shortened and flattened as with the Asian female previously described. The whole face can be widened with methods discussed in the chapter on corrective makeup. Such a rough border character will probably have long sideburns and a heavy black mustache like that illustrated.

While the characters of the 16th century Italian *commedia dell'arte* are usually made up in broad, comic fashion—Harlequin in white-face (see ahead: Clowns), and Pantalone and Il Dottore in vivid, absurd colors—they can have the straighter golden-olive complexions and heavy eye makeup described above.

MIDDLE EASTERN
AND ARAB

Characters:	Pharaoh, Cleopatra, fortune teller, gypsy
Foundation:	Olive-brown greasepaint or cream makeup, followed by a golden-tan cake
Highlights:	Tan grease, cream, or cake, lighter than foundation
Shading:	Dark red-brown grease, cream, or cake
Lips and cheeks:	Dark rouge outlined with dark brown liner or eyebrow pencil for lips
Eyes:	Dark brown liner or black kohl pencil

Makeup notes

You can get a swarthy Middle Eastern effect, B, with plain olive-brown grease, cream, or cake foundation and appropriate highlight and shading colors.

But the Arabic and Middle Eastern complexion has a special golden duskiness that requires a slightly more complex foundation mixture. To simulate that golden surface patina, first apply the olive-brown grease or cream as base. Powder thoroughly, then apply a thin layer of the gold or tan cake makeup, using a sponge. With the olive-brown base showing through the golden patina, you imitate the special lustrousness of the native complexion.

For the modern Middle Eastern or Egyptian woman, use moderately strong eye makeup, preferably with special black kohl eye liner, although normal dark brown or black will serve. Outline the lips in dark brown, then fill with dark red. The same dark eyes and full, dark red lips are common to the modern male, but should be less vivid.

Our knowledge of ancient Egyptian makeup comes from vase and wall paintings and indicates the formalized, cat-like eye makeup usually used for such characters as a pharaoh, A, or the famous queen, Cleopatra. Outline the upper and lower lids heavily with kohl or black, then emphasize with blue or even purple eye shadow extended all the way up to the outer eyebrow line. Lips can be red or a purplish hue or even green outlined in fine yellow pencil.

A gypsy fortune teller would have the same golden-dusky complexion and dark eyes, but if she is older, the foundation would tend to be more olive-brown and less golden, and liner and highlight should be used to add the lines of old age.

An Indian woman may wear a red mark in the center of the brow just a bit above the eyebrow line.

A harem girl might have exotic touches of glitter held in place with spirit gum on the outer edge of the browbone under the eyebrows, or even on the eyelids. Use mascara heavily on both lower and upper lids and add exotic eye shadow of blue, purple, or green.

NATIVE AMERICANS

Characters:	Black Hawk, Pocahontas, Sacagawea, Crazy Horse, Geronimo, Squanto
Foundation:	Florid and tan; a combination of yellow-browns with strong, deep red tones
Highlights:	Beige-yellow
Shading:	Strong red-brown
Lips and cheeks:	Medium-red
Eyes:	Brown eye shadow, brown eyebrow pencil

Makeup notes

There is a wide variety of facial types among Native Americans and skin color can vary from sallow to dark brown. But most Native American complexions have a predominantly red-brown or mahogany tone. Several makeup manufacturers offer foundations especially for Native American makeup. If you mix your own, experiment with small amounts until you get the right balance. The red or copper undertone should just show through the dusky, brown-skinned look, but the red should not dominate.

To simulate the prominent nose ridge and high cheekbones of the Plains people, A and B, emphasize hollows with shadow, prominent features such as cheekbones with highlight. Narrow the eyes by lining inside and close to the roots of your natural lashes, extending the lining an eighth of an inch beyond the outside corners of the eyes.

The Southwestern Pueblo tribes as well as many West Coast tribes and Eskimos have wider, rounder faces. To make your face rounder, apply principles described in Chapter 3.

For exposed hands, arms, and other body surfaces, select a liquid body makeup matching the red-toned foundation.

Ceremonial and decorative warpaint varies with the tribe and individual. The most commonly used colors are traditionally charcoal black, clay white, elderberry red, ochre, and the yellow earth colors. Discreet use of warpaint is usually more effective. Rather than splash color all over the face, try a lightening-like slash of yellow diagonally down the face, or emphasize a single design theme like the white finger-dots favored by the Sioux, Rain-in-the-Face.

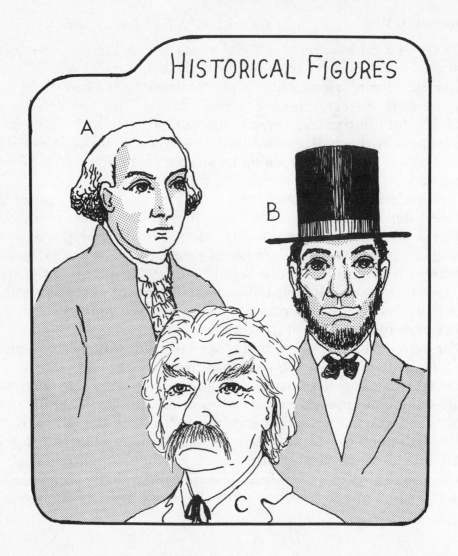

HISTORICAL FIGURES

Characters:	George Washington, Abraham Lincoln, Florence Nightingale, Emily Dickinson, Mark Twain, Amelia Earhart, Madame Curie
Foundation:	Light tan mixed with florid or pink for Lincoln and Twain; creamy for Washington; peach or pink mixed with small amount of ivory for the women
Highlights:	Lighter than foundation

Shading:	Pale brown for Lincoln and Twain; lake for Washington, Dickinson, Nightingale, and Curie; warm light brown for Earhart
Lips and cheeks:	Men—pale pink rouge, medium red or lake lipstick; women—dark or medium red lipstick and medium red rouge
Eyes:	Brown eyebrow pencil; brown eye liner; brown mascara for women; brown or lake eye shadow for men, blue-gray or dark mauve for women

Makeup notes

Makeup for historical and literary characters can be realistic—absolutely accurate representations of contemporary paintings or photographs of the subjects. Or it can be a form of caricature, emphasizing the character's better known features. Most stage representations end up being a combination of both.

It is best if the actor's facial characteristics are close to those of the character to be represented. Look for an actor with the bony angularity of a George Washington. Abe Lincoln had a long face with a wide mouth and strong cheekbones. For such characters as Florence Nightingale, of whom there are few reliable likenesses, look for a face suitable to the character's age, ethnic background, etc.

From that point on, you can often rely on one or two outstanding features: Washington's hair with its winged sides and ribboned queue at the back; Lincoln's squared black beard with no mustache; Mark Twain's flowing white hair, walrus mustache and shaggy, uplifted eyebrows; Emily Dickinson's pale complexion; Amelia Earhart's short curly hair. Good period costuming helps a lot as well as careful sculpting in light shadow and other makeup details. You can even include latex prostheses such as the meaty nose and long ears of Lincoln, Washington's straight, slightly arched nose, and Twain's hawkish nose and the heavy bags that developed under his eyes in his later years.

Characters:	Father Christmas, Wise Man, King Midas, Zeus, Father Time, Uncle Sam
Foundation:	Pink mixed with small amount of ivory, florid
Highlights:	Ivory
Shading:	Medium brown or lake
Lips and cheeks:	Bright pink or medium red rouge; light red lip coloring
Eyes:	Medium brown eyebrow pencil, medium brown or lake eye shadow

Makeup notes

This is makeup to represent hearty, healthy old age. Block out natural eyebrows with soap or clown white if necessary. The false nose recommended for Uncle Sam, A, can be built up with nose putty or mortician's wax (see Chapter 6) or can be a false nose made of papier mâché or latex. Attach it with spirit gum. For Father Christmas, B, and Uncle Sam, apply the pinkish, florid foundation evenly, except for areas where a crepe wool beard must be attached. Make up eyes and lips, then sculpt with highlight and shading, using methods described in Chapter 6. Next, add facial lines in highlight and shade, keeping them to a minimum. Frost eyebrows with white, or add wisps of crepe wool hair. To add to the impression of pleasing good health and vigor, use a sponge to lightly stipple the nose area and cheeks in medium or bright red. For hair and wigs, consult Chapter 4. For beards, see Chapter 5.

DECREPIT OLD MEN

A

B

Characters:	Silas Marner, Scrooge, King Lear, Pantalone
Foundation:	Florid pink-red; sallow yellow or ivory for ill-health
Highlights:	White or ivory
Shading:	Olive-brown or lake for Lear, touch of blue for Scrooge
Lips and cheeks:	Olive brown; pale pink with touch of blue for ill-health
Eyes:	Dark brown liner, light blue eye shadow

Makeup notes

Follow Chapter 6 directions for old-age makeup. The same chapter has instructions for Scrooge's beak-like nose, which can be built up with putty or wax or can be a papier mâché or latex false nose held in place with spirit gum.

The character differences between Scrooge, A, and Lear, B, determine the overall coloring. Scrooge is a sour person and liverish, hence the sallow, yellow complexion with hints of sickly blue in the shadows that hollow the cheeks, under the eyes and in the seamed lips.

Lear's complexion has a ruddy pinkness that complements his flowing white beard. Frost the eyebrows with white cake or clown white. You can add to the wild look of the eyebrows by adding stray wisps of white crepe hair, held in place with spirit gum. The eyelashes can also be frosted with white mascara or white cake applied with a mascara brush.

The basics of the Scrooge makeup can also be used for such gnomish characters as Rumpelstiltskin, and Doc or Grumpy of *Snow White and the Seven Dwarfs*. The same principles can be applied to the makeup of wrinkled old men, Pantalone and Il Dottore, for example, described earlier in this chapter (see "Latins and Mediterraneans").

WITCHES

Characters:	Three witches from Macbeth; witches from Hansel and Gretel; Halloween witches
Foundation:	Sallow yellow or ivory
Highlights:	White or ivory
Shading:	Olive-brown
Lips and cheeks:	Dark red, possibly a touch of blue
Eyes:	Dark brown liner, heavy mascara, possibly light blue eye shadow

Makeup notes

Makeup can vary from the broadly comic makeup, B, to a more realistic and threatening old hag, A. The same methods for aging described in Chapter 6 apply, with the comic witch makeup calling for more extreme coloring: a large false nose, a thrusting false chin, and a comically wild wig. The comic witch can have a basic foundation of clown white or bluish-white. The nose might even have a touch of purple.

For a wart on nose or cheek, attach a bit of puffed rice to the skin or false nose with spirit gum. Model it to shape with nose putty or mortician's wax, then cover with a darker color than the foundation, and use a touch of lighter highlight on the tip.

Eyes can be made up darkly, with deep, shaded sockets and heavy black brows. Black or dark brown crepe wool hair can be added to make the eyebrows more scraggly. Or, the eyebrows can be frosted with clown white or white cake for a more hoary look.

Characters:	Pinocchio, Cyrano de Bergerac
Foundation:	Warm tan or olive, tan and ivory
Highlights:	Pale tan or ivory
Shading:	Dark tan or dark brown
Lips and cheeks:	Strong medium-red rouge; dark red or lake lip color
Eyes:	Dark brown or gray eye shadow, brown liner, brown eyebrow pencil

Makeup notes

Pinocchio, A, is a marionette, so his foundation can be either ivory for a clown-like, unreal look, or tan to simulate the wood he is made of. The natural eyebrows can be blocked out with clown white or soap under the foundation, then quizzical V-shaped eyebrows drawn in with black or dark brown pencil. On the cheeks draw cheek blushes in strong red rouge, almost perfectly circular. The lines indicating his hinged jaw are drawn on with pencil over the foundation. Dark lines can be paralleled with light highlight lines, as with any facial lining. Each time the boy-puppet tells a lie, his nose grows. The noses of increasing length can be modeled in papier mâché or made of latex. They can be changed offstage, or with practice, onstage. The shortest nose is not attached until the last minute before the actor goes on, so that the spirit gum remains tacky. By turning away and working swiftly, the actor can remove the shorter nose and replace it with a longer nose which has also been prepared with spirit gum that is fresh and still just tacky enough to hold the nose in place but to give when it is pulled away; a risky bit of business, but it is possible.

Pinocchio's wrists and ankles should be made up with the same foundation color as the face. The wrist joints can be drawn in with pencil and white gloves may be worn.

Edmund Rostand's poet-swordsman, Cyrano, B, is also distinguished by his enormous nose. Apply foundation, highlight, and shading as you would for any straight makeup job. The goatee and mustache can be hair pieces or built with crepe wool hair.

Cyrano's nose is built with putty or mortician's wax on a plastic thimble affixed to the top of the actor's nose with spirit gum and thin strips of adhesive tape. Once the thimble is secure, the nose is modeled over it by pressing small quarter-inch balls of putty or wax into place, taking care not to dislodge the thimble. When there is enough bulk for the nose (and to hold the thimble in place), begin modeling around the base to attach it firmly to the skin. Continue sculpting with your fingers and a clay modeling tool. Finally, sponge makeup in place to match the foundation, then brighten the nose with tones of pink and red.

A new thimble nose must be built for every performance. A false nose of papier mâché or latex will do nearly as well.

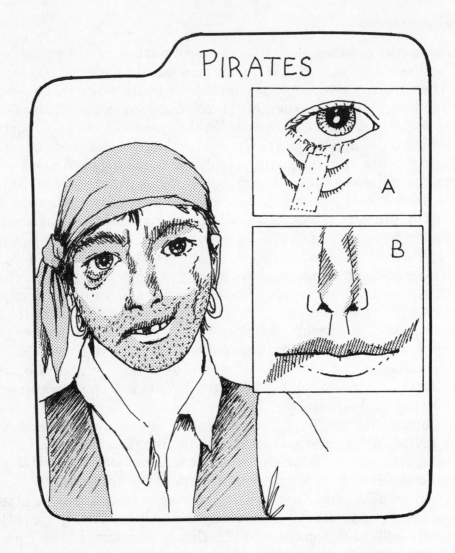

Characters:	Long John Silver, Captain Hook, robber, vagabond
Foundation:	Pink or olive-brown stippled with florid and lake
Highlights:	Ivory or pale yellow
Shading:	Olive-brown
Lips and cheeks:	Dark red or lake
Eyes:	Red or brown eyebrow pencil, brown eye shadow, red liner for bloodshot effect

Makeup notes

This makeup will do for any rough, tough type.

Your purpose is to create the effect of a dirty, rough skin: First apply an olive-brown foundation evenly, then use a sponge to stipple it finely with dark brown cake or black face powder. For a more florid complexion like that of Long John Silver, mix pink into the olive-brown, then stipple that foundation with red-brown or red cake makeup, particularly on and around the nose to simulate broken veins.

Insert A shows a method for making one eye droop ominously. Use a strip of transparent tape to pull the lower pouch of one eyelid down, as shown. Conceal the tape with the addition of more foundation and highlight it to make it look puffy.

To make eyebrows bushier, add wisps of black and white crepe wool hair. Add small red dots at the inside corners of the eyes for a bloodshot look. That angry look can be increased with the addition of a ¼-inch length of red above the black eyelines at the outer corner.

For the broken nose effect, see insert B. Begin with a strong swath of highlight down the bridge of the nose, curving it into an "S" shape. Then use shadow and more highlight to model and blend. A plug in only one nostril will add to the impression the nose is twisted.

The mouth can also be given a twisted look by distorting the lip line, as suggested in insert B.

For an unshaven jaw, stipple in dark brown or black or make myriad tiny ¹⁄₁₆-inch marks with a very sharp eyebrow pencil.

A more realistic way to create the effect of a stubble beard is to snip crepe wool hair into ¼-inch bits, then apply spirit gum to the beard area, allowing it to become tacky. Then take a pinch of the clippings between thumb and forefinger and dab them onto the gummed skin, trying not to let your fingertips touch the gummed surface. Continue to apply the clippings until you have the desired texture.

Blacken the teeth with black greasepaint painted over with a thin coat of spirit gum. Or use black crayon or black tooth wax.

Scars can be painted on in light and shadow. Collodion can be brushed onto the skin; it draws and wrinkles the skin to a scar-like texture, which can then be touched up with makeup. There are also ready-made latex scars available from makeup suppliers.

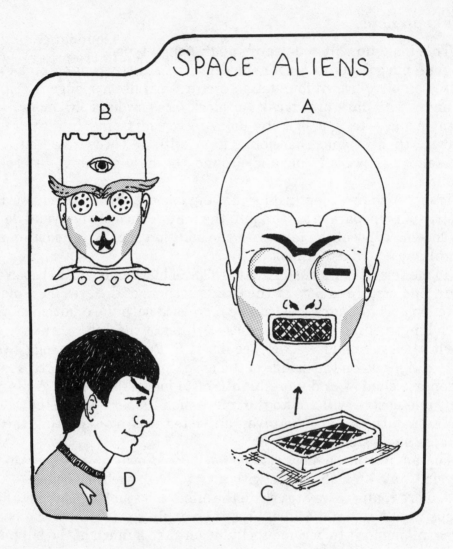

Characters:	Robots, Spock
Foundation:	Medium green; blue-white for Spock
Highlights:	White or yellow
Shading:	Gray, blue, or dark green
Lips and cheeks:	Pink rouge, silver, white, black, blue
Eyes:	Goggles, ping pong balls, strainers; for Spock— medium blue eye shadow, black eyebrow pencil and liner

Makeup notes

For the alien, A, apply a fluorescent green cake foundation. Actors with sensitive skin will be better off using a non-fluorescent medium or light green cake, liquid, or greasepaint foundation.

Block out the eyebrows with soap or clown white. Apply the foundation as usual, but cover the outside corners of the mouth and the blocked-out eyebrows. Add yellow or white highlights to the cheekbones, but do not highlight or shade the nose. Use medium gray or deep green to shade under the cheekbones and narrow the face so it seems to squeeze down toward the mouth. Draw the eyebrow shape with dark brown eyebrow pencil, then fill in with black or dark blue.

The eyes of this alien are made from halves of ping-pong balls with slits cut in the fronts. Attach them with nose putty mixed with spirit gum, running a bead of the mixture around the edge of each eye shell, then pressing it firmly into place. Make sure the slits are large enough for you to see and move safely about.

Alien A's mouth is made from a plastic soap dish sprayed silver and glued to a sheet of starched gauze, C, with an opening in the gauze to allow you to breathe and speak. This prosthetic piece is attached by brushing spirit gum to the area around your mouth and to the inside perimeter of the gauze, allowing both to become tacky, then pressing the mouth piece into place. Blend the edges of the gauze with foundation.

Alien B's head piece is made from a pasteboard box with a section of egg carton glued on top. The eyes are small plastic strainers held in place by a putty and gum mixture, as above, or rigged with elastic and worn like welder's goggles. (Goggles or strange dark glasses can also be used for alien eyes.)

Alien B's winged eyebrows are made of ironed green or blue crepe wool hair glued in place with spirit gum, and stiffened with acrylic hair spray *before* attaching to the face. Apply foundation to the outside corners of the mouth, then paint on the design.

The Spock look-alike makeup, D, uses a blue-white foundation, pale yellow highlights and gray or dark blue shading. Block the natural eyebrows before the foundation is applied. Highlight and shade to give the face a long, narrowed shape. Draw in the angled eyebrows with brown outline and black liner. For the pointed ears, see Vampires in this chapter.

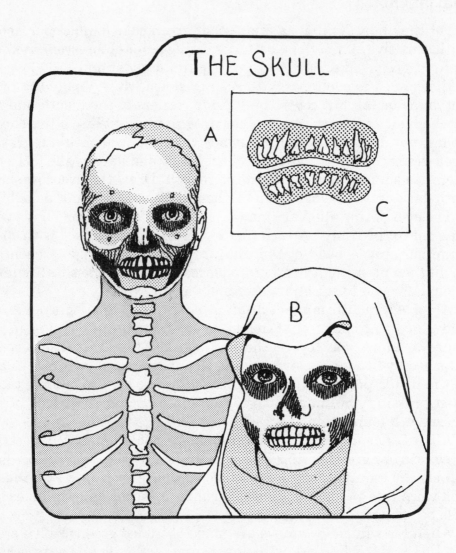

THE SKULL

Characters:	Death, the ghost of Hamlet's father, skeleton
Foundation:	White or ivory
Highlights:	Sallow ivory or light yellow
Shading:	Black, dark brown
Lips and cheeks:	Black and white; touch of yellow on teeth
Eyes:	Black grease, liquid or cake; touch of bright red eyeliner or grease

Makeup notes

This makeup can be simple, as in B, or more complex, as in A.

For the easy version, the top of the head can be masked with a hood, although the hair should be pulled back tightly and secured with pins. Cover the entire face and neck with a foundation of white or ivory greasepaint, liquid, or cake; powder once. Draw the dark areas with a light brown eyebrow pencil then fill them in with black. If your foundation is ivory, you can add white highlights on the brow and points of the cheekbones. The black nose area is a triangle with an open notch in its bottom, as shown. The teeth are drawn on around the mouth in black, as shown. A touch of yellow to each tooth shape helps. A dot of red at the inside corner of each eye adds to the spooky effect.

For a more realistic makeup, A, you need a skullcap. A tight, white bathing cap will serve, but you will have to use nose putty or mortician's wax to smooth out the hem of the cap where it joins the skin, then cover the skullcap with greasepaint. A plastic beachball the size of your head can be cut to fit over your head and ears. Professional latex bald-head caps are available from theatrical supply houses.

The cap must be painted to match the sallow ivory or white foundation and the edges carefully blended. Next, fill in the dark areas of eye sockets, nose, and under the cheekbones, as indicated in the illustration. Use dark brown shading to model the edges of the dark areas as they blend into the white, bony prominences.

The teeth can be painted in, as with B, or you can make three-dimensional sets of teeth, upper and lower, out of mortician's wax or the yellow wax wrapped around some cheeses. Cut the two gum shapes from starched gauze or nylon netting, as shown in the inset, C, then press the teeth into the gauze or glue them in place with spirit gum. Paint them, then affix upper and lower teeth into place on your upper and lower lip areas, using spirit gum to secure them. Blend more foundation over the gauze or netting to hide the edges.

Add the fine lines on the skull dome in sharp eyebrow pencil and the tiny sinus holes in the bone above and below each eye.

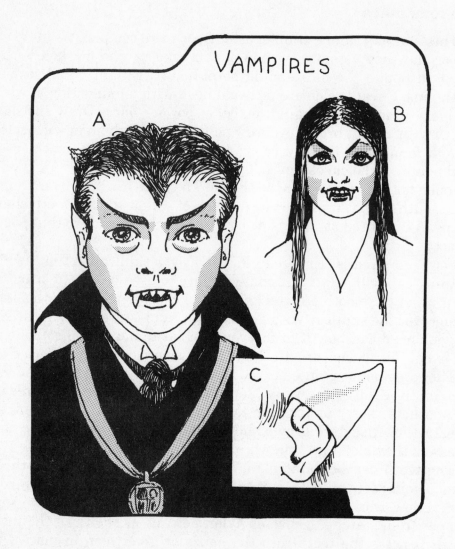

VAMPIRES

Characters:	Count Dracula, Halloween vampires
Foundation:	Cream-sallow mixed with green or medium gray
Highlights:	White or light yellow
Shading:	Medium green or gray
Lips and cheeks:	Dark blue or dark green; dark pink rouge
Eyes:	Black eyebrow pencil; black liner
	blue or green eye shadow

Makeup notes

The color scheme for the makeup of the Count, A, and the vampire shown, B, can lean to green or to blue. It is best to decide beforehand which, then to select shading and eye shadow colors to match.

First, block out the ends of the eyebrows with soap or white paint. For the foundation, mix a light flesh color such as cream-sallow with small amounts of white, then add the medium gray, green, or blue until you get a color that is pallid and tinted with the green or blue rather than dominated by it.

Apply the foundation until it is smooth and unstreaked, then begin to sculpt in highlight and shading, using the light yellow or white to highlight the tops of the cheekbones, the bridge of the nose and the point of the chin.

Next, shade with green, gray, or blue under the cheekbones and at either side of the temples. Use black cake or greasepaint to darken and deepen the eyesockets. Use an eyebrow pencil to strengthen the eyebrows, tilting them upward at the ends. Outline the eyes with dark brown or black liner, apply mascara to lashes, and touch the lids with hints of metallic blue or green.

Red ⅛-inch dots at the inner corners of the eyes or very thin lines of red along the lower lids create a blood-thirsty look.

By far the best vampire fangs are the plastic sets sold around Halloween and available year round from novelty stores and theatrical supply houses. You can make fangs from candy chewing wax or the wax wrapped around yellow cheese, attaching the false teeth to a framework of pipe cleaners cut to fit inside the mouth between the lips and gums. Or you can build a set of teeth: cut teeth from white or yellow plastic and attach them to pink dental wax available from your dentist or some drugstores.

Count Dracula's hair is combed straight back in the middle-European manner. It can be darkened with brush-on temporary hair color and silver-white streaks added. To produce the suggestion of satanic horns, spray with clear hair spray; while it is still tacky, tweak wisps of hair into a subtle suggestion of horns. Vampire B can wear a long black wig.

The Count's lips can be made up with dark blue, dark green, or black. For B, the lips should be painted fuller than the natural outline and in blood-red, with a hue of blue or green added. A trickle of stage blood or red greasepaint can be added at the corner of the mouth for a particularly grisly effect.

Pointed ears for vampires, C, can be purchased ready-made or fashioned from papier mâché or latex. Attach them with spirit gum, then add makeup to match the foundation.

Characters:	Frankenstein's monster, werewolf
Foundation:	White mixed with blue
Highlights:	White or pale blue
Shading:	Medium blue
Lips and cheeks:	Blue or red for lips, a hint of rouge for cheeks
Eyes:	White for lids or latex lids, black eyebrow pencil and liner

Makeup notes

On a sheet of glass, mix white and blue to make a pale blue foundation for Frankenstein's monster. Or mix on the face, blending thoroughly and covering the lower lip. Add highlight and shading to broaden and shorten the nose and deepen the hollows under the cheeks, extending them down close to the corners of the mouth, as though the cheeks were sucked in.

Make the top lip as thin as you can in blue or medium red. Leave the lower lip the foundation color.

For the high, bulging brow, find a cardboard box that will fit your head and cut it out as shown, B, and in the auxiliary illustration, A, B, C, and D. Make sure it fits snugly around the backs of your ears and that the tab between the eye arches fits down onto the bridge of your nose. You can add a rounded brow ridge over the eyes with plastic wood or mortician's wax sculpted on the box. Glue black crepe wool hair in place, adding touches of hair spray along the front and side fringes, then twirling the crepe hair into points to give the ragged, artificial look. You can add a mortician's wax incision down the brow, with metal or paper clamps to add to the impression the monster was clamped together from spare parts. Glue silver- or gold-painted spools as electrodes at the side of the head box, as indicated.

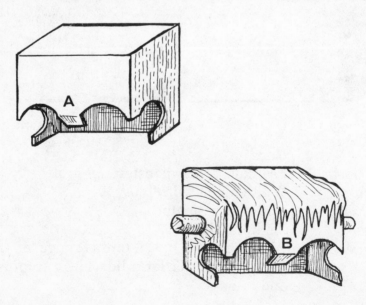

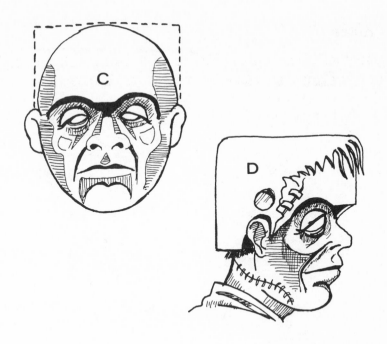

Make up the lids in white and slant the black liner lid line as shown, to simulate the heavy, hooded eyes. Better yet, make bulging lids from adhesive tape, as described in "Asian Male," earlier in this chapter. Or make them from liquid latex, as described in Chapter 6. Paint them in white or medium blue with blended highlights of white or pale blue.

Make up the hands and wrists in the pale blue foundation color, then draw and highlight stitched wrist lines. Use spirit gum to attach metal or paper clamps across the wrist lines to indicate the hands have been attached.

The werewolf (inset) is a challenging exercise in the application of crepe wool hair (see Chapter 5). Note that the hair sweeps back from a point just above the nose and that it extends well up onto the cheeks. Use Halloween fangs or teeth made from wax or plastic. Use a mixture of yellow and brown hair, brown foundation for what little of the face is left showing. Broaden the nose and make it up in yellow with pink highlights. A prosthetic nose can be made from papier-mâché or liquid latex (see Chapter 6) and stuck in place with spirit gum.

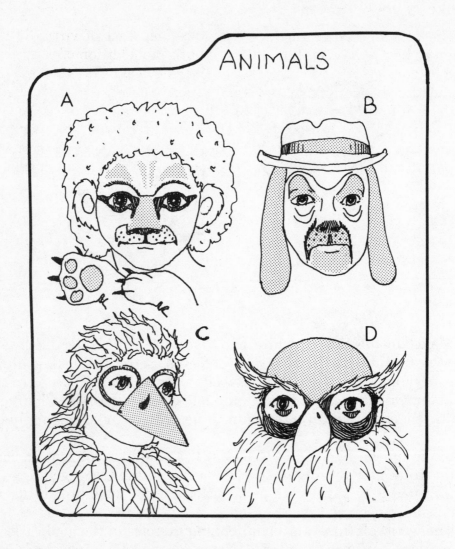

Characters:	Cowardly Lion, Hound, Enchanted Bird, Wise Old Owl
Foundation:	Assorted
Highlights:	White, ivory, pale yellow
Shading:	Medium brown, dark brown, or lake
Lips and cheeks:	Assorted
Eyes:	Dark brown or black eyebrow pencil, assorted eye liner and eye shadow colors

Makeup notes

The human face can be made to resemble that of virtually any animal, bird, and even fish or insect with the addition of prostheses and clever use of paint, wigs, and other devices. Aim not for exact replication, but for just enough suggestion to encourage the audience to enter into the fantasy. Good acting and voice work will do the rest.

The lion shown, A, wears a tawny orange wig, false fuzzy ears and cloth paws as well as a papier mâché or latex nose piece. The muzzle is painted in above the mouth, the forehead striped with orange or yellow, and the eyes heavily made up, as shown.

The hound, B, has a latex prosthetic nose and upper muzzle, and ears of false fur. The face can, in fact, be entirely painted on.

The bird, C, has a false paper nose and wears a hood and cape made of a ski hood with feathers of assorted colors stuck into the fabric.

For the head of the owl, D, the large papier mâché beak fits over the actor's nose and the rest of the actor's face extends below and behind a broad feathered cape. A purple skull cap is worn and the huge outside area of the eyes is an eyeglass-like mask constructed of painted cardboard with feathers glued in place as the winged eyebrows.

There are, of course, latex and papier mâché casque masks that cover the entire head and are realistically sculpted to resemble animals. But aside from limiting vision and being dangerous, these can be so "realistic" the audience isn't inclined to enjoy them at all. The secret to good animal makeup is to show enough of the human underneath, and thereby blur the distinction between the animal and the actor.

CLOWNS

Characters:	Pierrot, Harlequin, the Tramp
Foundation:	Clown white greasepaint or stick; or white cake
Highlights:	White, if any
Shading:	None
Lips and cheeks:	Bright, strong reds, assorted other colors
Eyes:	Black liner and mascara for whiteface, assorted colors for others

Makeup notes

The first clown white makeup was probably white clay or chalk. Modern clown white uses assorted ingredients. Zinc cream, available from pharmaceutical supply houses, makes an acceptable white clown foundation when mixed to suitable consistency with cold cream.

The traditional whiteface clown, or Pierrot, A, is now seen mostly in European circuses. First block out the eyebrows with soap or spirit gum (see Chapter 3). Next, apply the white foundation with fingers or sponge. Although this white expanse invites all kinds of wild coloring, the secret of good whiteface makeup is moderation. A few eccentric feature changes lend a strange beauty; too much turns the face into a reckless patchwork. In the Pierrot makeup the eyes are elaborately but realistically made up, with blue lids, heavy lining, and a few large lashes drawn at the outside corners. The quizzical false eyebrows are first outlined on the forehead with brown eyebrow pencil, then filled in with bright green. One or two triangular tears are drawn below the eyes and filled in with yellow. Or, a single drop-shaped tear located under only one eye could indicate the clown's inner sadness. Then, a single round dot is filled in with red-orange on the tip of the nose. The lips are outlined in the bow shape shown and filled in with red, highlighted with a touch of gloss on the lower lip.

Female clowns often wear huge false eyelashes, B, which can be cut from paper and stuck in place with spirit gum.

The tramp and buffoon clowns, C and D, were developed in American circuses. The familiar tramp makeup made famous by Emmett Kelly is not copied exactly by other clowns, out of respect for its inventor. However, designs similar to the one shown have been used. The foundation is flesh-colored, not flat white. This enables some modeling with ivory or cream highlights and brown shadow. The red nose can be papier mâché or latex and glued in place, or built up with nose putty. The unshaven effect is accomplished with a coarse sponge and black or dark brown grease, cream, cake, or liquid black.

The buffoon or grotesque clown, D, requires a white cloth skullcap to which tufts of bright orange crepe wool hair have been attached with spirit gum, and then drawn to permanent peaks with dabs of gum. The eyebrows have been blocked out and the high, arched upper "eyelids" outlined then filled in with green, blue, or purple. The mouth is outlined in brown or dark red, then filled in with scarlet. Most fantasy and buffoon clowns wear bulbous false noses. A false nose can be made quickly from a single section of papier mâché egg carton held in place on the face with elastic, see B, below. Or, cut a triangular hollow in a small red rubber ball (or ping-pong ball painted red) and hold it in place with elastic, A. Another nose, C, is rigged with a tiny light bulb inside, and a fine wire running to a set of batteries and a switch. The batteries and switch are then concealed in the clown's pocket, and the nose can be made to blink on and off. The nose shell must be made from a hollow red ball of plastic translucent enough for the light to shine through.

Big noses can also be built up with nose putty or mortician's wax, then colored with makeup. False latex ears are sometimes used, or you can make your own ears seem bigger by using wads of nose putty or wax behind them to press them forward.

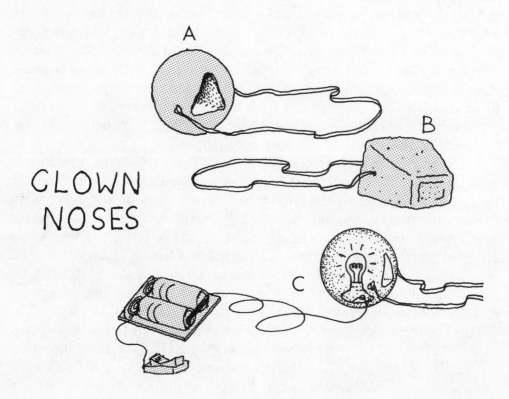

CLOWN
NOSES

APPENDIX
Characters in Makeup Gallery